Praise for

I SAW THE ANGEL IN THE MARBLE

WHAT A BLESSING it is to see, in print, the wisdom and wit of our dear friends, Chris and Ellyn Davis. For years they have been our first stop when we are looking for solid, trustworthy advice on how best to train up our children. Their timely articles have made a huge difference in our home and in the learning process of our children—now 20, 17, and 14. The Davis' heart for the Savior and their willingness to follow Him down the ancient path will impact generations yet to come.

—VALERIE MCDANIEL
Homeschooling Mom

HOW EXCITING! You no longer have to wait for Chris and Ellyn Davis to come to your conference. Now you can access their vast amount of experiences and practical advice any time you want. This is destined to be the most often used, dog-eared book on your bookshelf and the one you recommend most often to your friends!

—CINDY WIGGERS, OWNER
Geography Matters

I

CHRIS AND ELLYN DAVIS CAN BE COUNTED ON to snag the genuine article from the overwhelming array of materials spread before bewildered parent educators. Their Elijah Company catalogue has been the ultimate field guide for parents purposed to growing children into adults who follow God-led paths educationally, vocationally and spiritually. For years the Davis' have generously given seasoned advice and counsel. Now readers can savor the best of their best in this wisdom-filled volume. Bravo and thank you!

—PAM VON GOHREN, AUTHOR
Across the Kitchen Table:
Observations About Children and Education
Minnesota's best known homeschooling Mom

POUR YOURSELF A CUP of hot tea, grab a pillow, and settle down for a quite evening with Chris and Ellyn Davis. You will find wisdom and comfort tucked between the pages of this book. Be prepared to take your homeschooling to a higher level; be prepared to be blessed.

—VALERIE BENDT, AUTHOR
Reading Made Easy
Unit Studies Made Easy

IT'S WONDERFUL to finally see all these great articles in one place. The Davis' philosophy is very similar to my own, and I'm sure most other *relaxed home schoolers* will be interested in this collection.

—MARY HOOD, PH.D., AUTHOR
The Relaxed Home Schooler

WHEN CHRIS AND ELLYN TALK, we listen! When Chris & Ellyn Davis write, we read! God has blessed these two with an incredible amount of wisdom—spiritually, philosophically, and practically. If we'd had a book like this when we began our home education adventure 20 years ago we would have missed numerous pitfalls. If you are just starting or if you need to get a fresh vision for being home with your family, you've got to read this book!

—BOB AND TINA FAREWELL, FOUNDERS
Lifetime Books and Gifts

CHRIS AND ELLYN ARE SOUGHT AFTER speakers and authors who are very dear to my heart. They have been ministering to home schoolers through their Elijah Company for many years. Their catalogs and newsletters have included not only their expert evaluations of excellent books and materials, but also some of the best counseling available. Now they have gathered their most useful articles under one cover. I feel strongly they will be a blessing to both you and future generations.

—JOYCE HERZOG
Speaker, Author, Consultant

CHRIS AND ELLYN ARE UNIQUE VOICES of wisdom in the homeschool movement. They've "been there, and done that." Over the years, they have contributed their wisdom at conferences and in their books and catalogs. Their overview of the different curriculum styles is particularly valuable. In a sea of "how-to" books about homeschooling, there are very few "why" books. Chris & Ellyn can help you understand why homeschooling is a great choice for your children - and give you a valuable orientation to what you need to know as you embark on the journey.

—ROB SHEARER, PUBLISHER
Greenleaf Press

III

CHRIS AND ELLYN CONTINUE TO ENCOURAGE the home-schooler's journey with articles that inspire and motivate. How blessed we are to benefit from their years of experience! Their personal journey brings expertise, wisdom of educational choices and options, and godly advice regarding our families. Consider *I Saw The Angel In The Marble* essential to your homeschool library shelf.

—DEBBIE WARD
Common Sense Press

IT'S ABOUT TIME that Chris and Ellyn put all their wonderful articles into a book. Their catalog has been a wealth of information for new homeschoolers for many years. It has been a must read. Now, it will be even better to be able to have their years of wisdom and encouragement in a book. Thank you Chris and Ellyn for finally doing this.

—DEBBIE MASON
Mother of four, ages 15 to 23
22-year homeschooling veteran.
Local & State leader for 17 years.

ELIJAH COMPANY

A COLLECTION OF ESSAYS

I SAW THE ANGEL IN THE MARBLE

by Chris & Ellyn Davis

ELIJAH PRESS

First Edition

Published by:
Elijah Press
1023 Eldridge Loop
Crossville, Tennessee 38571
www.ElijahCompany.com
1.888.235.4524
1.931.456.6284

Some of the anecdotal illustrations in this book are true to life and are included with the permission of the persons involved. All other illustrations are composites of real situations, and any resemblance to people living or dead is coincidental.

This book incorporates content originally published in the Elijah Company EJournal, Copyright © 1991-2004.

Unless otherwise identified, all Scripture quotations in this publication are taken from the HOLY BIBLE: NEW INTERNATIONAL VERSION® (NIV®) Copyright 1973, 1978, 1984 by International Bible Society, used by permission of Zondervan Publishing House, all rights reserved.

Cover and interior design by Frank McClung, Drawing on the Promises LLC, www.drawingonthepromises.com

Printed in the United States of America
First Edition.
ISBN 1-884098-24-x

FOR RESOURCES, CONFERENCES, TRAVEL AND COUNSELING
PLEASE CONTACT ELIJAH COMPANY,
CALL 1.888.235.4524 (USA)
OR 1.931.456.6284
WWW.ELIJAHCOMPANY.COM

Dedication

THIS COLLECTION OF ESSAYS is dedicated to…

…all you Pioneers who endured the misunderstanding and anger of family, friends and neighbors; the possibility of going to jail; and your own nagging insecurities, in order to take back your God-given responsibility to raise your own children, when doing so meant that you stood alone against an entire culture. Though most of today's homeschoolers will never know you, you know who you are. You have done something that has generational—and, yes—even eternal implications.

…the Moores, the Harrises and the Colfaxes who went before the Pioneers and said that the journey was worth the trouble.

…the prophet, Jeremiah, who taught us that just because everyone is doing something, doesn't mean that God thinks it's right. Jeremiah told us to:

> "STAND AT THE CROSSROADS AND LOOK.
> ASK FOR THE 'ANCIENT PATHS'.
> WHEN YOU FIND THEM, WALK THAT WAY
> AND YOU WILL FIND REST FOR YOUR SOULS."
>
> (JEREMIAH 6:16)

CONTENTS

FOREWORD

AS CHRIS AND ELLYN DAVIS gently lay out their case for home-schooling in the book you hold, *I Saw the Angel in the Marble*, the absence of shouting and rhetoric, and their tangible respect for the reader, might cause even the best of readers to miss the uniqueness of the Davis argument: that it is the *home* in homeschooling which requires the emphasis, not the *schooling*.

Although I've personally perused over two hundred titles on the subject in the past twelve years, many of them moving accounts of individual and family insights, many of them valuable additions to modern wisdom and literature, I can't recall ever hearing so forcefully a thesis which to the academically trained specialist seems so counter-intuitive; that the very specific, very particularized context of one's own family is the only place "to become proficient at the specific giftings, talents, and callings" which God (or Nature if you're a secularist) had placed in each individual child.

It is a contention which immediately resonates with me, and with the experience I gained over thirty years with some four thousand young people as a public school teacher in New York City. Put simply, those students who liked and respected their parents—and it was never difficult to tell which ones they were—invariably did well for themselves at everything, displayed courage and resilience in the face of adversity, inspired others, including myself, and seemed to love the truth—while those who were indifferent to, or actually disliked their parents (always the majority of my classes, but dramatically increased as a proportion among the children of the prosperous), seemed to stagger from one small crisis to another. Even among the self-confident, they were visibly uncomfortable *with themselves*, always looking for some way out. Out of what, you might ask? Out of everything I would answer; they had no peace within their skins, no faith in anything but "winning," no hope that dreariness could be avoided except through moments of high sensation: sex, drugs, high grades, violence, action, and, of course, winning—often at any cost.

Although I never put it as clearly as the Davises do, working to repair industrialized families—the artificial proletariat of the mass consumption age—became my secret weapon as a schoolteacher. I could never share that with colleagues or supervisors because to both groups parents were the enemy (sometimes that seemed to be the chief topic of complaint in the Teachers' Room!), I began to visit homes regularly talking to parents, usually mothers but sometimes fathers, too, about their kids *as individuals*.

I tried to convince them that in the forty-five minutes a day that I had their sons and daughters, they were crowded in with thirty other boys and girls, everyone a stranger to me with no other relationship possible to us, yearlong. We were doomed to superficiality no matter how much we liked one another.

But here is the point: *they were not so limited.* If we could work cooperatively, with them as the team leader where their own children were concerned, then their superior understanding of their own flesh and blood, and of the ancestral streams speaking through the young, would give us a fighting chance to create an individualized curriculum for each one. The project worked better than I could have dreamed, problems became challenges—and almost always manageable. And my life as a schoolteacher bloomed. I looked forward to each day with the kids, even the "bad" kids.

Chris and Ellyn—and the rest of you—naturally have a huge advantage over my own situation. You actually live alongside your children many hours each day, with the opportunity to constantly and intensively observe each one until you can see what God created and put inside them. You're able to control the schooling part so it doesn't drive the family apart. You can keep the Fear which is so much a part of institutional education out of the young imaginations.

What *Angel in the Marble* can do is to give you a model of the good attitude needed to succeed at homeschooling, along with an armload of practical advice, advice seasoned through long experience. It deals with real needs, proper environments, types of difference, materials, the ancient paths, and much more. I wish the opportunity had been there for me to read this book long ago when I began teaching, but I'm glad it's there for you—after all, you and your kids are my neighbors!

I don't mean to be inflammatory, but government schooling has made people dumber, not brighter; has made families weaker, not stronger; has ruined formal religion with its hard-sell exclusion of God; has set the class structure in stone by dividing children into classes and setting them against one another; and has been a midwife to an alarming concentration of wealth and power in the hands of a fraction of our national community. We've had enough of that way of training up children. Chris and Ellyn have a better way. Let me suggest that when you've finished this brave book you discreetly leave it in your local day care center as a lifeline for some fellow soul to grasp.

—*John Taylor Gatto*

OXFORD, NEW YORK
APRIL, 2004
WWW.JOHNTAYLORGATTO.COM

XI

Acknowledgements

WE WISH TO THANK...

...the thousands of homeschoolers who have looked to us these many years to help them raise their own children in their own homes. You have refused to accept the prevailing cultural notion that price is the only relevant issue in doing business with someone, but have continued to insist that business is a relationship. We have enjoyed serving you and continue to look for more ways we may serve you in the future.

...Vivian Adams and the crew that is "Elijah Company" who take the calls, ship the orders, give counsel, work at paying the bills, make mistakes and try to fix them.

...Kathy Clement and Judie Kowles, our bulletin board moderators, who tirelessly answer the same questions over and over and never lose patience with those who need encouragement and counsel. You have been an invaluable resource to many faceless homeschooling parents.

...Frank McClung who left the security of the worldly order to enter the security of a faith walk with his God, and who has served us in the areas of our eNewsletters, our catalog and everything artistic.

May God reward you all for your faithfulness and courage in being part of this effort to serve a future generation!

—*Chris & Ellyn Davis*
Elijah Company, Inc.

INTRODUCTION

THE ARTICLES THAT APPEAR in this book have been written over the course of many years. They represent a journey several of us "old timers" have taken since the early 1980's as we have attempted to raise our own children and reassume the responsibility for every aspect of their lives. The articles have appeared in our Elijah Company catalog or have been sent to the over 20,000 families who subscribe to our electronic newsletter. You may even have seen some of them before as, throughout the years, many have been reprinted in whole or in part in other newsletters or periodicals.

For a long time people have asked us to put these articles in one place so they would be easier to find, easier to read and easier to make available to friends. So, finally, we did it. Our apologies for having taken so long!

This book represents the best of 15 years of Elijah Company articles. Although we made an attempt to arrange the articles in some logical order, feel free to junp in anywhere—or ignore some altogether. Our hope is that what you read will offer real practical help. We would love to hear from you. You may email us at chris@elijahco.com.

May the Lord bless you as you raise the next generation!

Chris & Ellyn Davis

I

ALTHOUGH HOMESCHOOLING IS ALLOWED in all 50 states, states vary widely in what they require for a family to homeschool legally. A little knowledge can be one of your greatest allies against either inadvertently breaking the law or having officials burden you with regulations which the law does not require.

Sometimes people in authority, ignorant of homeschool laws and not approving of homeshooling, place demands on homeschooling families that are simply not required by the state's law.

The Homeschool Legal Defense Association web site [www.hslda.org] is a great source for current homeschooling laws, news and information. You can go to their site, enter your location and print a copy of your state's homeschooling law. You can also find the homeschooling organization in your area or state.

State and area homeschool leaders are your best source for local homeschooling information, although we still recommend that you obtain a copy of your own state's homeschooling law. One last comment: We have said that in all 50 states homeschooling is allowed. However, some homeschoolers do not believe the State has any authority over the area of homeschooling. The philosophy here is that the

State has no authority in any area where the Lord has told someone what He requires. Therefore, if the Lord has told a family to homeschool, attempting to follow a state's legal guidelines to be considered a "legal" homeschooler is the same thing as recognizing that the State has authority in this area of life. Further, whenever a person or family asks the State's permission to do what God has already told them to do,

> SOMETIMES PEOPLE IN AUTHORITY, IGNORANT OF HOMESCHOOL LAWS AND NOT APPROVING OF HOMESHOOLING, PLACE DEMANDS ON HOMESCHOOLING FAMILIES THAT ARE SIMPLY NOT REQUIRED BY THE STATE'S LAW.

that person or family is giving the State the right to say "No," thereby telling a family it cannot do what God has already told them to do.

Many of us began homeschooling in the early 1980's when there were no homeschooling laws and some of us faced arrest for following our convictions to homeschool. Because of these convictions we were prepared to go to jail if that was our only alternative to doing what we believed the Lord was mandating.

Our advice to new homeschoolers is this: If a family can homeschool following the State's homeschooling requirements and can do this without violating the family's conscience, this is preferred to taking an adversarial position toward those in authority. The problem arises when a State's compelling need to have an educated populace meets the God-given authority of parents and the parents determine that the State has overstepped its authority in telling parents what they must do with their own children.

This will be different with every family; and, when the family decides that the State has gone too far, that family should be prepared for whatever battles lie ahead.

The Home School Legal Defense Association has provided legal protection for thousands of homeschooling families over the years, has saved parents thousands of dollars in legal fees, and has kept others out of jail. No family should attempt to homeschool without at least becoming familiar with what HSLDA has to offer.

2

AFTER TWENTY YEARS of homeschooling our children, we have seen homeschooling evolve from a misunderstood underground movement to a political and economic force. Years ago, when a friendly check-out clerk would ask our children why they weren't in school, they would answer, "We homeschool." At that time, almost no one knew about homeschooling and the few who did were opposed to it. Nowadays anyone you talk to knows someone who homeschools. It has become an acceptable and respected alternative to traditional schooling. Why do parents homeschool their children? We'll explore some of the reasons parents are choosing to educate their children in the home.

REASON 1 | SOCIAL

The most common question asked during the early years of the homeschooling "movement" was, "What about socialization?" For those unfamiliar with the concept of socialization, the question was directed at the notion that children must spend a lot of time with their peers so that they will grow up having learned how to properly interact with others in various social contexts. If a child is removed from daily interaction with other children his age the kind of interaction typically

4

found in a public school setting will not that child grow up socially stunted and harmed for life? This remains one of the major fears voiced by relatives of homeschooled children.

In appreciation of this concern, researchers began to take a serious look at the well-accepted idea of the necessity of peer socialization. Homeschooling parents had already begun to write articles supporting

---

**CHILDREN WHO SPEND MORE TIME
WITH ADULTS BECOME BETTER
SOCIALIZED THAN CHILDREN WHO
SPEND MOST OF THEIR SOCIAL
TIME WITH THEIR AGE-MATES.**

---

the opposite contention: that spending a lot of time with one's own age-mates actually harm children by making them peer dependant, unable to think and act independently, and causing them to grow up with an unhealthy need for peer approval. The Bible seems to support the idea of peer dependency when it states that foolishness is bound up in the heart of a child; and that the companion of fools himself becomes a fool.

What researchers found and what homeschooling parents have long contended is that children who spend more time with adults become better socialized than children who spend most of their social time with their age-mates. This is true mainly because, when a child spends a lot of time with adults, the child is having modeled to him or her a far more mature set of social skills.

Researchers found that the homeschooled child is more involved with other children than most people assume. Homeschooled children are involved in an average of five activities outside the home for which they seem to have plenty of time since they watch only about 1/10th as much television as public schooled children. The homeschooled child will score well above his age-mates in every available self-esteem and socialization test. Perhaps this is why two-thirds of homeschool graduates end up self employed, a direction that takes a great deal of self esteem.

The real question one should ask is not, "What about socialization?" All children will be socialized. The question that should be asked is, "By whom do we want our children socialized?" Who will teach them their social skills? With whom should they spend most of their time: adults or peers?" Some homeschooling parents are even beginning to ask friends who send their children to public school, "Why send your children to public school; aren't you concerned about socialization?"

REASON 2 | MORAL

One of the reasons children should be socialized mainly by their parents is that the moral foundation of one's life is laid through hundreds of small interactions on a daily basis. This is true for the laying of either a good or a bad moral foundation. Normally, the older the individual the more he or she has acquired a realistic life perspective, including the need for a life lived within the boundaries of moral principles. Even a relationship with God can be immature or mature, and spending time with mature, godly adults is critical to establishing a godly foundation in life. It just makes sense that children should spend most of their time with their own parents if those parents want their children to grow up with a godly life perspective.

The question is often asked, "If other children could be an improper influence on my children, shouldn't I completely shield my children from the influence of others?" This idea is a popular teaching in the Body of Christ today. However, I disagree with it.

Having raised four children into adulthood, I think the answer to this is a qualified, "No." Our boys have had the opportunity to spend a great deal of time with other children and adults. Some of them have been downright ungodly people, adults and children alike. But, the influence such individuals have had on our boys' lives 1) has helped our boys to clearly understand the consequences of sin because they have seen it in other's lives; b) has shown them why none of us wants to have to deal with such consequences; and, c) has shown them just how badly Christ is needed in the lives of those with whom we come in contact and how our lives can affect others for good.

THE MORAL FOUNDATION OF ONE'S LIFE IS LAID THROUGH HUNDREDS OF SMALL INTERACTIONS ON A DAILY BASIS.

As a father, I have always tried to go with (or take) my sons into whatever relational context they have entered, especially until I was assured they had internalized a strong moral foundation. I have wanted them to know that the father's presence is always with them, no matter where they go. Also, a father's continual training in ways of godliness is crucial. One vital example is the necessity of training our children to responsibly relate to members of the opposite sex.

REASON 3 | SAFETY

This is a delicate issue today. Suffice it to say that more and more parents are becoming fearful for their child's safety in public schools.

Although this was a concern even when I was in high school in the 1960's, violence is increasingly becoming a way of life in America, including in our schools. I know a superintendent of schools who had been a principal in an upper, middle class neighborhood for many years. Recently she told me that, when she began as a principal, a successful day meant that her pupils had spent the day getting an education. By the time she left the principalship, a successful day meant that her pupils had made it through the day without being physically harmed.

The issue of safety is not limited to our children's physical well being. Emotional and spiritual safety are, undoubtedly, of greater real importance than being concerned about the potential of my child being shot before the end of the school day.

REASON 4 | CONTEXTUAL

John Gatto former New York City and New York State teacher of the year states that public school-style education separates a child from the daily context of life. By this he means that to live life successfully, one must, in the process of growing up, gain an appropriate set of "life-preparing" experiences. Public education not only does not provide enough of these experiences, it fills a child with information and experiences that actually must be overcome for the child to become a success in life. Says Gatto: "Schools school; life educates."

Most education is theoretical knowledge. "You will need to know this one day, so you'd better learn it now," works fine for some children. If a child is able to catalog thousands of pieces of information for future use, has a good memory, or simply has a learning style that fits the way public schools teach, that child will do well. Other children do not do well at all. These are the children who need to interact with what they are learning (feel it, touch it), or interact with other learners, or need the information to have some realistic application.

One reason why homeschoolers do so well in college and why more and more colleges are aggressively recruiting homeschoolers is that children taught at home tend to have a more real-life approach to learning. They have not spent large amounts of time doing busy-work. Learning has real meaning to homeschoolers. Here is a somewhat lengthy quote from John Gatto which says it all,

> *"...the natural sequence of learning is destroyed without experience (hands-on experience) "primary data" (to give it an academic title), must always come first. Only after a long apprenticeship in rich and profound contact with the world, the home, the neighborhood, does the thin gas of abstraction mean much to most people. ...only a few of us are fashioned in such a peculiar way as to thrive on an exclusive diet of blackboard work and workbook work and bookwork work and talkwork work of all sorts. When we fail to take into account how most children...learn by involvement, by doing, by independent risk-taking, by shouldering responsibility, by intermingling intimately into the real world of adults in all its manifestations...we have created the mise en scene where a mathematical bell curve seems to describe a human condition in which only a few children have any real talent."*

REASON 5 | IDENTITY

> *"Due to its emphasis on competition, institutional education leaves a large population of losers, damned to the self-concept that they cannot succeed no matter what they have a heart to do."*   *John Gatto*

God gives each of us an identity: a specific "who we are" as well as

9

"what we are to do." There are no "generic" children. Public schools function as if there were no other kind. Many seem to succeed in a public school setting. But what is this "success" that they attain? Is it the ability to attend a college of their choice? Do they learn what they need to know to succeed in life?

It now takes almost six years for a college entrant to obtain a traditional four-year degree because the average college student changes majors more than twice. He enters college not knowing why he is there and, while there, tries to find out what he wants to do with his life. What a waste of time, energy and money!

IS IT POSSIBLE THAT WE ARE TRYING TO EDUCATE CHILDREN TO DO SOMETHING OTHER THAN WHAT GOD CREATED THEM TO DO?

Forty percent of college entrants drop out. They discover that college cannot give them an identity. They have no reason to be there. Only about 15% of those who do graduate college end up working in the area in which they got their degree. Again, what a waste of time, energy and money!

What's wrong here? Is it possible that we are trying to educate children to do something other than what God created them to do? If we are honest, can we admit that we are really focused on training children for the job market? Is that what education is really all about? Dr. Joel Spring, Professor of Education, has written, "The educational goal of preparing citizens for participation in a democracy has been replaced by that of preparing them for employment."

And, what about those who do not succeed in public school? Why don't they succeed? Could it be that we are trying to run children through an educational process created for the "Every Child" when there is really no such person? We give each child a name. But, why not just call every boy, "Boy," and every girl, "Girl?" Better yet, why not call every child "Person" since this is the way they are going to be treated in their institutional school setting: "You are Person; and, like all Persons of your same age, you will be offered a generic education created for Everyone."

There are two things a child must be given in order to become truly good at what is in his heart to do (translate: what God has put in this child to be manifested to his/her generation). They are Time and Resources. Public schools cannot individualize education so that students are treated as other than "generic children." Yes, public schools offer Electives the opportunity for an individual to take courses that have specific interest to him or her. Yet, if each person is uniquely gifted for a specific life work, that individual must be given some very specific "tools of the trade" as well as a lot of time to spend becoming good at his/her talents or callings.

In Paul's letter to the Ephesian church, Paul says that we were created to accomplish certain works which God, Himself, planned, in advance, for us to do. None of us are generic human beings.

REASON 6 | THE REAL GOAL OF PUBLIC EDUCATION

Let's be honest. In today's society the end product of all education is: A JOB. When asked why we are putting all this knowledge into our children's heads, the real answer is, "We are preparing our children for employment."

Most homeschooling parents are expecting their children to end the education process either by moving right into the job market or on to a college where the degree obtained will provide them with a better job. A few days ago I received an email from a homeschooling mother. In part it said:

> *"My son graduates from home school this year and I wanted to know what your son did after graduation. We have a local Jr. college, but my son doesn't really know if this is what he needs to do...he is an outdoorsman...loves animals and hunting...I need some advice on what some possibilities are for a godly young man who has been homeschooled since 1st grade. He 'dreads' taking the SAT I...."*

Can you hear the concern? This child is about to graduate and he hasn't yet declared what he is going to do in life!

The day before receiving this email, my wife and I had a conversation with our middle son, James. My oldest son, Seth, always had a pretty good idea of who he was and what he wanted to do in life. James, however, had graduated from 'high school' the previous year and was still not sure what he wanted to do. James is a serious-minded, godly young man who had a part-time acting job. James had been sharing with his mother how he was struggling with being 18 years old and still in the process of discovering who he was in the Lord and the direction of his life. At this point my wife said, "Son, very few people are ever given the freedom and time to find out who they are and what that means for their future. Most just go get a job, only to discover later that they have spent years doing something that is not really what is in their heart to do. What your Dad and I want to do for you is give you a most precious commodity: Time. You will leave us soon enough and we will never again have the kind of relationship with you that we have now. We are not in a big hurry for you to leave the home life we have all enjoyed together. What we do want is for you to come to terms with what the Lord has placed in your heart. For most people this takes some trial and error. The best gift we can give you right now is time. There is nothing magical about graduation from high school. It doesn't mean that your education is over. What education means to us is finding out what God has created for you to do and then having enough experiences to be good at that."

Not long after this conversation, the Lord sovereignly brought into James' life an opportunity to attend a very special college in California. After two years in this school, James discovered his real love: working with children. What if we had not trusted the Lord to bring to James just what He needed at just the right time. Or, what if we had not given God the time to open James' spirit and reveal to everyone what He had put into James to be expressed to his generation.

REASON 7 | ESCAPING THE MYTHS

These myths are not actually taught. Rather, they become internalized truths because they are the driving assumptions on which public education is based and we all grow up within these assumptions. [For a more thorough development of the mythology of public schooling, you will need to read John Gatto's book, *A Different Kind of Teacher*]. I will share two myths that our family has tried to overcome in our over 20 years of homeschooling.

Myth 1 | A student's success depends solely on his own abilities and accomplishments. Public schools are set up as if each student has entered a cross-country track meet. The course will take 12 years and, for each participant who reaches the finish line, there is a reward (a diploma) that says he has finished the race. If he is one of the top finishers, he may also enter a subsequent race that may take several more years. The rules of the race are that he must always remain in his own lane. Races are not cooperative efforts and he will not be allowed to turn aside and find out from the other runners how this race should best be run.

This is a myth because it does not in any way mirror real life. In real life those who succeed do so because, throughout their lives, they find ways to learn from those who are running or have already run the same race. Therefore, to forbid students from interacting with one another in the learning process (including the taking of tests), is to teach them that success in real life is a solo flight. On the contrary, learning is a cooperative endeavor and no one gets to the end having done very well who must rely solely on his own abilities.

Myth 2 | Failure is permanent. Every course, every test, is a one-time. The results are permanently cataloged as if our very future depended upon our ability to download thousands of facts into short-term memory and bring them up at will.

This myth also does not mirror real life. America used to be a nation of risk-takers who led the world in discoveries, inventions and entrepreneurial ventures. Today, so many adults are driven by a fear of failure, risk-taking has all but disappeared. Twelve years of School has taught us that failure is a "permanent record issue" keeping us from future success. We avoid failure by not taking risks. However, not only is failure one of the main reasons real leaders are successful (failure is, after all, our best teacher); but, God says that those who walk with Him simply cannot fail.

REASON 8 | FINANCIAL

The government estimates the cost of providing a year's worth of public school education to be about $5,500.00 per student. However, the estimated cost per student of a year of homeschooling averages less than $500.00. This cost difference is made the more remarkable when reading Reasons 5 & 6, above.

REASON 9 | EDUCATIONAL

There is a great disparity in the educational outcome of homeschoolers and public schooled students. Here are a few statistics:

On nationally standardized tests, the average public school student scores at the 50th percentile. Taking the same test, the national average of homeschoolers' scores will be at the 85th percentile.

A public schooled student's standardized test scores are affected by differing demographics that have no affect on the homeschooled child. For instance, the parents' educational and income levels; the gender of the child; the child's race; and whether or not the child's teachers are certified and/or college trained all affect the child's standardized test scores. However, none of these factors affect a homeschooled child's test scores, which will remain around the 85th percentile even if the child is a poor, minority male whose parents are neither educated nor certified teachers. This is remarkable!

Also, statistically, the longer a child remains in the government school system, the less well he or she will do academically. By the time the average American child graduates from high school, he or she will do less well on standardized tests than his or her peers in almost every other industrialized nation in the world.

REASON 10 | SPIRITUAL

The contemporary homeschooling movement began mainly as a religious movement. As public schools were forced to ignore, then remove references to, and finally refute the spiritual foundations of our nation, godly parents began to wonder about other venues for educating their children. As courts required a separation of Church and State not fathomed by the Founding Fathers, parents realized the need to take possession of their children's upbringing not experienced since the pre-Industrial Revolution days of the mid-1800's.

Most government leaders want their populations to be healthy, happy and educated. When America was a young nation, its populace was industrious, hard working, and highly literate. In the 1840's the Industrial Revolution began and a flood-tide of emigration moved

WHERE DO ACADEMICS FIT AMONG ALL THE OTHER PRIORITIES OF LIFE?

toward our shores. This concerned our government because many of those seeking the "good life" in America were not well educated, nor did they consider education a high priority. American educators and government officials became alarmed for the future. If an educated population is one of the main reasons a country is successful and prosperous, what would our nation's future be like if its population was not well educated?

At this very time, certain members of the federal government introduced the novel idea that the State should consider its youth, "Children of the State," rather than children of their parents. The rationale behind this thinking was that children grow up to become the adults who make a country weak or strong and it is obvious that not everyone knows what it takes to raise a child who will end up contributing positively to the nation.

Soon, certain leaders began to postulate that parents, especially parents who were Christians, were actually hindering the potential for their own children. By the last 19th century, parental influence began to be seen as conflicting with governmental child-rearing ideals. Compulsory school attendance laws were aimed at separating children from their parents so that new experiments of child rearing could be tried.

[We suggest a reading of the books, *A Different Kind of Teacher* and *Going Home to School* for an insider's opinion of what really drives government education].

Here is the progression: The Government decides that an educated populace is required. Government then mandates an educated populace (and even determines what is included in that education). Government determines that education should be the time-priority for children between the ages of six and eighteen. Given that children "belong to the State in a more real sense than they belong to their parents," the Government's priorities rule. Children are taken from their families and placed in the Government's educational system. The rightness of all this has not been questioned for over 150 years. Until now.

It is homeschooling parents who are asking the questions, "Where do academics fit among all the other priorities of life?" "As our children grow up, is it our primary goal to provide them with an academic education?" "Who knows my children well enough to provide the kind of education each one needs, the State or the parents?" If God is suggesting that there are higher priorities than academics if there is a "bigger picture" than just making sure my children have a State-approved education we had better find out what this "bigger picture" is!

By saying that I am homeschooling for "spiritual" reasons, I am saying that I am raising my children to become members of a culture other than the one in which we live out our natural, daily lives. Yes, my children must have an education that will fit them to function in the 21st Century; but, I am primarily raising them to function in the culture known as the Kingdom of God. In the past, government schools had this same priority; today, they do their best to make sure this is not even part of a child's experience in school.

REASON 11 | RELATIONAL

Not long after my wife had written the book, Going Home to School, our family was attending a homeschool conference as book vendors. In her book, Ellyn had explained some of the history of public schooling in America and shared why we, and so many others like ourselves, came to the conclusion to homeschool our children.

During the conference, a man walked into our booth. He was frustrated, confused, and agitated. He approached Ellyn and blurted out, "Tell me: just why you are homeschooling your children!"

I was standing behind Ellyn and smiled at the man's question. I thought, "Of all the things Ellyn wrote in her book, what would she choose to say to this guy?" I quickly thought of what I might say had he asked me instead of Ellyn. I will never forget what Ellyn told the man that day. She didn't say anything from her book at all. She simply said, "I don't know if I will be able to pull this off; but, when it's all said and done when my boys are all grown and have left home what I really want is to have had a relationship with them. It seems to me that if they are gone from me, all day, every day, the chances of that happening are not as good as if they are at home with me". The man responded, "That's what I needed to hear," and he walked away.

REASON 12 | FOR THE FUTURE

In every city and town across America groups of insecure parents are raising their own children while other parents are sending their children to the government schools. The work of these parents is mostly hidden to the rest of society which, anyway, is largely indifferent to their efforts. Many of these families have internalized a vision of their children becoming just what God intended them to become. They wonder why every set of parents don't see the obvious benefits of homeschooling.

As the world grows darker and more dangerous by the year, God's work is being done in a corner, as He prepares a generation for a day that is impossible to imagine. We parents may be taking it "a day at a time," (always wondering if we are raising a bunch of misfits); but the truth is that God is giving us just enough faith so that, if we are willing to hear Him and do something not done for over 150 years, this generation will emerge from our families with an uncomplicated faith in their God, an unmoveable disagreement with Darkness, and an unmistaken sense that they were born for such a day as this.

Statistical information for this article has been taken from material produced by the Home School Legal Defense Association (www.hslda.org) and the National Home Education Research Institute [www.nheri.org].

3

WHY DID WE CHOOSE to home school our children? Over the years, as I have been asked this question, I've usually spouted off reasons such as: "We want the freedom to select teaching materials that reinforce our religious beliefs and moral standards. We want to provide the academic superiority of a one-on-one teaching situation. We want the ability to monitor our children's socialization experiences. We want to tailor the course of study to the individual. We want the flexibility to create more family time." These are the reasons I clung to as I tried to convince our family, friends and even curious strangers that we were not really crazy for keeping our children out of that traditional and highly revered American institution—the public school. I, oh so seriously, would list these reasons and add a few statistics and stories about the success of home schooling so that my decision sounded very rational and well-informed.

But, when I'm perfectly honest with myself, those are just secondary reasons why I chose to teach our children at home. The real reasons are matters of the heart. Home schooling was and still is attractive to me in part because of the images it evokes: children snuggling on the couch as I teach them to read; little boys' faces alight with excitement as they assemble model rockets; my son absorbed in a book while lying on the back of his pony; cross-country trips in the station wagon learning about the Oregon Trail; acting out the battle of Yorktown with boys who have muskets slung over their shoulders; twilight adventures collecting lightning bugs; the pride in a child's voice as he says, "Look how well I wrote these letters!"

IN THE END, NO MATTER WHAT THE GENERATION, TEACHING OUR CHILDREN AT HOME HAS LITTLE TO DO WITH ACADEMICS OR WITH SHIELDING THEM FROM SECULAR INFLUENCES.

To me, home schooling speaks of close family relationships, highly valued home and family life; happy children who love learning; meaningful traditions; simplicity; nurturing, mentoring relationships; restoration of excellence; freedom to pursue individual interests; entrepreneurship; recapturing meaning and purpose to life; and discovering one's destiny.

Our home schooling journey is now completed. During the past twenty years we have seen a profound shift in home schooling as well as in our culture at large. We grew up in an era when there were very few latch-key kids, where neighborhoods were fairly safe because you knew all your neighbors and they shared many of your same values, and where families were far less stressed and far more stable. In other words, we grew up in homes where there were parents present most of the time we were home. But we are seeing a whole new generation of parents embarking on the home schooling adventure who don't come from that base of home and family.

Many of you come from homes that were filled with tension or with various forms of dysfunction. Your image of a father may be a busy, negative, pressuring, authority figure, and your image of a mother may be a distant, distracted, but somewhat nurturing career woman. Or perhaps you don't have any strong images of a particular parental role because you come from a broken home. The other difference between your upbringing and ours is that your lives were lived primarily in a series of institutions: daycare, school, after-school care, church, recreation centers. As a result, you may be not only disconnected from a sense of real family, but are also disconnected from a sense of meaning and purpose in this life. A large reason home schooling is so attractive to your generation is that it carries with it the promise of providing the family-oriented feelings, experiences, and identity shaping you missed as children.

But what we all have in common is the desire to make right some wrong in the upbringing of children—not just for ourselves, but so that our children can have the type of home life we believe is possible, but may never have experienced. We all long to restore something that has been lost. In this case what has been lost is the heart of the parents for their children and the heart of the children for their parents. We home school because we want to reconnect to multi-generational values, to relationships, and to a sense of destiny.

So, in the end, no matter what the generation, teaching our children at home has little to do with academics or with shielding them from secular influences. It has a great deal to do with our desire to turn both our own hearts and theirs. And we turn hearts not by the pushing, demanding, shaming, or competition of an institutional setting, but through the drawing out of true identity in an intimate, open, trusting, emotionally safe, relational environment that we try to create in our own homes.

4

SEARCHING FOR THE ANCIENT PATHS

YEARS AGO WHEN WE first began thinking of home schooling, the Lord challenged us with Jeremiah 6: 16: "Stand at the crossroads and look, and ask for the ancient paths and the good way." At the time, we realized we hadn't a clue what God's ancient path or good way was for educating our children. Both of us had been for the most part raised by institutions, for the school and church had claimed the majority of our waking hours as children. And these institutions had taught us a way of looking at and living life that was not necessarily God's way. We took up God's challenge to "look" and "ask" with questions like:

How do I see myself? We came to adulthood at a time when many Americans considered themselves victims of one sort or another: victims of their upbringing, of their environment, of their lack of education, of the prejudices or actions of others. Unfortunately, we shared the victim mentality's sense of entitlement and unwillingness to assume personal responsibility for our actions.

What is the focus of my life? Because we were Christians, we automatically would answer, "God is our focus, of course!" But in reality our focus was on the principles and protection of God. Our interaction with God was more a contract than a relationship. We wanted to put Him in our theological box and we expected Him to respond if we followed certain Scriptural principles and engaged in certain spiritual activities.

What is education? We had been taught that "knowledge is power," and an education is a commodity— something you acquire in order to make you more powerful, either through a better job or a higher social status.

Our public school upbringing had steeped us in a noble humanism that made us the center of the universe and judged everyone and everything else according to whether or not it benefited us. We were firmly enthroned as the gods of our own lives and carried that "me, me, me" mentality into our Christianity. Even Jesus was, in a way, a commodity, because our faith centered around how God would satisfy our needs and help us achieve our ambitions. It was quite a shock to realize that it isn't the ungodliness in the world that threatens our children, it is the ungodliness in us! This startling discovery strengthened our determination to search for God's ancient paths and good ways.

We can't presume to say that we have "arrived," but at least we can share with you some of what we have discovered on our journey.

PREPARED FOR A WORLD THAT NO LONGER EXISTS

Both of us grew up in the 50s and went to high school and college in the 60s and early 70s. Those of you who did not live through the 1960s have no idea of the radical shift in American culture during those years. In the 50s, our life was lived pretty much as it had been lived for generations. Fathers worked at the same job for years, mothers usually stayed at home and raised their children, and neighborhoods were places where everyone knew everyone else and you and your neighbors shared the same values and many of the same religious beliefs. Picture "Leave It to Beaver" and "Father Knows Best" in your mind and this will give you a pretty good idea of the kind of life we were being prepared to live. Then came the 60s when all traditional assumptions were challenged: assumptions about life, about family, about what had value, about what was worth believing. Instead of being told to work hard, do well in school, get a good job, and raise a family, we were told: "Turn on, tune in, and drop out." Millions of young people did. The whole world suddenly changed and as we reached our late-20s, we realized we had been prepared for a world that no longer existed. The benchmarks, the anchors, the external goals, and the institutional structures that were an important part of our parents' lives were no longer reliable. Our high school and college degrees and our family backgrounds were little help in dealing with the capricious job market, the confusion about roles and relationships, the cynicism and disillusionment, and the relativistic values that greeted us in the world of adulthood.

As we now prepare our own children to function in a future that may be as drastically different from today today is from the '60's, we ask ourselves these questions: How can we give our children the tools and abilities to survive and thrive no matter what the future may bring? What skills and knowledge will stand the test of time and be valuable to them as adults? What helped us weather the ups and downs of the last thirty years? What of all we learned from childhood through adulthood was "real?"

PUTTING IN THE BIG ROCKS FIRST

In *The Seven Habits of Highly Effective Families,* Stephen Covey has you imagine a man standing behind a table. On the table are a large glass jar and a pile of rocks. The man fills the glass jar to the brim with rocks and asks you, "Is the jar full now?" You answer, "Yes." The man then brings out a container of small pebbles and begins putting them into the jar. The pebbles fit in the spaces between the big rocks and you see that the jar was not really full. Even though it was full of rocks, the jar still had room for pebbles. The man asks, "Is the jar full now?" You answer, "Yes." The man then filters quite a bit of sand through the pebbles and big rocks. You think that surely the jar is full now, but the man shows you that there is still room for more by pouring a glass of water into the jar. The jar that you thought was full with just rocks wound up holding pebbles, sand, and water as well.

IT WAS QUITE A SHOCK TO REALIZE THAT IT ISN'T THE UNGODLINESS IN THE WORLD THAT THREATENS OUR CHILDREN, IT IS THE UNGODLINESS IN US!

Our time is like the jar in Stephen Covey's story. It can be filled with quite a lot of big things and little things. But the important lesson from the story is: Put the big rocks in first. If we don't make sure we do the really important things, the "big" things, our lives can easily become filled with the "smaller" things. Covey says we spend our time in four ways:

[1] On things that are urgent and important (crises, emercies, big problems)

[2] On things that are important but not urgent (planning, renewing our vision, thinking, developing relationships, studying, moving towards achieving our goals)

[3] On things that are urgent but not important (most interruptions, phone calls, some meetings)

[4] On things that are neither important nor urgent (useless recreation, watching TV, procrastinating, piddling).

To be productive, successful home schooling parents, we need to be spending more and more of our time on activities that are the most important. Those activities are the "big rocks" while the other activities fill our lives with pebbles, sand, and water.

DETERMINING YOUR EDUCATIONAL PHILOSOPHY

Home schooling parents are often told they should determine their "educational philosophy" before they make any decisions about how they will home school. This may be helpful, but it is not essential, because our "educational philosophy" tends to evolve as we become more knowledgeable about what we are doing and about the real needs of our children. Plus, the concept of having an "educational philosophy" tends to make us think in terms of home schooling as a compartment of our lives instead of as a lifestyle. Our recommendation is that you begin your home schooling journey by doing the following four things:

First, examine the viewpoints and teaching approaches that currently influence home education. If there is a particular emphasis or teaching approach that appeals to you, take the time to learn about it. The fact that it appeals to you may be the Lord's gentle nudge in that direction.

Second, take a long, hard look at the presuppositions and objectives of institutional education by reading books such as *Going Home to School and Dumbing Us Down*. Why? Because, as Pogo said, "We have seen the enemy and he is us!" We are so used to thinking of school as children sitting in desks, listening to lectures, and working on pre-packaged curriculum for six hours a day, 180 days a year, over a period of twelve years, that we have a hard time imagining any other way. Also, many products for home educators are merely repackaged versions of public school materials, and we need to be able to recognize them as such. Otherwise, we unwittingly find ourselves adopting the same scope and sequence, the same methods, and the same standardized curriculum that was derived from the public school's presuppositions and that seeks to achieve its objectives. We will worry if our children aren't reading by the time they are six or doing fractions by nine. We will guide our children toward popular careers. We will feel unqualified to teach without an education degree. In short, until we understand the misconceptions behind public schooling, we will think that traditional institutionalized education is true education.

For most of us, our public school upbringing has steeped us in ideas about education that have to be discarded if we want to effectively educate our own children at home. As John Gatto says, "School was a lie from the beginning, and it continues to be a lie." If we know no better, we may buy into the lie and perpetuate its thinking.

Third, try and get in touch with your family's convictions and values and the real needs of your children. Once you have an idea of what you really want for your children, you will be better prepared to chart your home schooling course.

Fourth, buy several home school resource books that give an overview of home schooling. These books will overwhelm you if you don't already have an idea of where you want to go with home schooling, so don't dig into them until you have some sense of your family's convictions and the real needs of your children. Start with books such as *Homeschooling the Early Years, …the Middle Years*, and *…the Teen Years*. They provide general information about teaching each age group. From there begin looking at curriculum guides like those by Cathy Duffey. Educate yourself about "what's out there" before you start educating your children.

Prepare to spend several hundred dollars and a few months getting clear about what you want to do. If it makes you feel any better about the amount of time and money you have to spend getting ready to teach your children, think of it this way: The average public school teacher has spent four to six years and twenty to fifty thousand dollars learning how to teach your children. Why shouldn't you spend some time and money preparing yourself?

However—and this is a *big* however—don't think that you have to have everything figured out before you begin. You can adapt as you go. So loosen up and accept the fact that some of what you try will be a total waste of time, energy and money. This is all a part of learning what works for you and for your children. Consider it payment of your tuition in Home Educating U.

5

THE OPTION TO HOMESCHOOL came to our attention as an alternative to the private school our church was attempting to form. As we looked into creating the church school, all the parents in the church decided instead to homeschool their children. The year was 1983.

During those early years of homeschooling, we dealt with several issues which are not as important today as they were then. We had to contend with relatives who questioned our sanity and with government officials who questioned our right to remove our children from the public school. But the most often asked question was, "What about socialization?"

Like most "movements" homeschooling has transitioned through several phases. As our friend, Rob Shearer has said, "The first homeschoolers were the Pioneers. Then came the Settlers. Now we are seeing lots of Refugees." Pioneers are people who begin to move in a direction because they have a "vision" which others do not yet see. Many homeschooling Pioneers only vaguely understood why they felt compelled to homeschool their children. They often had trouble communicating as to why they were driven to do "such a radical thing." As a consequence, they often had to withstand censure from those they loved;

and constant threats of harassment or arrest from authorities. Yet they moved forward through these difficulties because they could not help themselves. They had a conviction that what they were doing was the right thing to do.

ARE YOU DOING THIS BECAUSE YOU HAVE A CONVICTION, OR BECAUSE THIS IS ONLY A PREFERENCE?

In the early days of homeschooling, none of the Christian publishers would sell products to a homeschooling family. These families had to figure out how to do everything themselves as well as create their own materials. They had to "make it up as they went." The phrase back then was, "Are you doing this because you have a Conviction, or because this is only a Preference?" What this question meant was that the courts would usually leave a homeschooling family alone if that family could prove they had a conviction to homeschool that kept them from sending their children to another kind of school.

If, on the other hand, they only preferred homeschooling to other forms of education, the courts tended to feel that preference was not enough reason to allow parents this choice. The Pioneers were being watched by many families who tended to agree with homeschooling, but did not want to make such a radical decision. Eventually, however, a large group of what we now call the Settlers came to believe in what the Pioneers were doing. By the time the Settlers became involved, homeschooling had become legal and many of the mistakes made by the Pioneers had been corrected.

The Settlers liked the lifestyle they saw being exhibited in Pioneer families. They liked the materials created by the Pioneers. They, too, began to have the conviction that this new/old way was the best, and perhaps, the only way to raise their children.

A few years ago, as homeschooling became an accepted alternative to both public and private schooling, parents dissatisfied with government schools and unable to afford private education began to withdraw their children from "school." An increasing stream of Refugees began to flood into homeschooling. Refugees want their children to receive a "traditional" (like the public school) education; but, for various reasons, they just don't want their children in a traditional school. These homeschoolers tend to have great difficulty homeschooling and that difficulty creates failure which, in turn, drives them to return their children to the institutional school.

What is the problem with a Refugee mindset? First of all, Refugees do not have a (positive) vision for homeschooling. Rather, they are focused on escaping something negative (school). Refugees do not have the conviction that drives the Pioneer and, usually, the Settler. Refugees do not want to learn what the Pioneers have to tell them. This is because they are homeschooling for a different reason than do the Pioneers. Refugees only want to know answers to such questions as: "Where can I purchase materials that work, are the cheapest, and require the least of me as the 'teacher'?" "Does the material look like public school material; will it accomplish the same ends as public school material; and will it keep my child on track with his public schooled counterparts?"

Unless Refugees become at least like Settlers, they will not realize that homeschooling is not just another way to educate one's children. It is a totally different way of living and relating as a family unit. It is a different way of looking at children and their futures and how we "get them there." In reality, homeschooling is just a part of the total picture of family life. This is why the kind of educational and social experiences found in what Pioneer homeschoolers call "the institutional school" cannot be easily replicated at home. We can't really (and mustn't) "bring the children home and their school along with them." Institutional schooling works best in an institution. It doesn't work very well in the home. If you are a Refugee and have read this article to the end (and this is the end), we recommend that you not stop here. Never allow yourself to stop learning how to do this thing we call "homeschooling." Attend seminars and get seminars on CD.

Remember: All it takes to become a Pioneer is to do what God tells you to do. And, all it takes for a Pioneer to stop being a Pioneer is to fail to move on with God.

Happy Homeschooling for the next generation.

6

AS WE HAVE SPOKEN with home schooling families across the nation, we are continually asked two kinds of questions. The first kind of question has to do with developing the lifestyle necessary to successfully educate our children at home: *How do I make it work?* The second kind of question concerns resources: *What do I use to make it work?* These questions are repeated in varied forms wherever we go.

Step 1   Count the cost.

Step 2   Begin with the end in mind.

Step 3   Develop a strategy.

Step 4   Create a context.

Step 5   Choose teaching materials.

These five steps are a progression of deciding what we want to accomplish and how we plan to do it, and each step builds on the last.

NEW HOMESCHOOLER?

We know how overwhelming it is to begin home schooling. A myriad of decisions must be made, and the choices in teaching materials seem overwhelming. Read the article, "Homeschooling Teaching

Approaches" (Chapter 8). If you feel a special kinship with a particular teaching philosophy, read books in that area. Here are some other suggestions:

The most important thing you can do is find out where your children are physically, emotionally, mentally, and academically. Start with where they are and build on that. Often children taken from a public school setting have problems with self-esteem, peer dependency, academic "burn out," and the adjustment from classroom to home. The most harmful thing you can do with a damaged child is jump right into academics. Take time to become reacquainted with your children, to "wash away" the institutional effects, to determine their learning strengths and weaknesses. You may want to just cover the necessities of academics (language arts and math) for the first few months to a year, then gradually add more subjects.

▣ Remember that teaching your children at home is going to be quite an adjustment for you as well as for your children. Take care of yourself. Don't over commit. Stay at home. Find ways to make your life easier.

▣ Beware of adult peer pressure. Many of your relatives and friends will criticize your decision to home school. Don't feel like you need to live up to their expectations. Other home schooling parents may pressure you to try their favorite curriculum or intimidate you with their children's achievements. Remember, you know your children's needs better than anyone else.

▣ Determine your philosophy of home education. If you don't have a firm belief that what you are doing is the right thing for your children, your commitment will waver when you are under stress (and you will experience stress!).

▣ Cultivate the attitude of a learner. Remember, home schooling is fairly uncharted territory. Look at failures as learning experiences. Try to laugh at the stupid mistakes you will make.

▣ Use what you have. Your finances and resources may be limited; your circumstances may be less than ideal. Instead of wishing things were different, look for ways to best use what you have.

MANY OF YOUR RELATIVES AND FRIENDS WILL CRITICIZE YOUR DECISION TO HOME SCHOOL. DON'T FEEL LIKE YOU NEED TO LIVE UP TO THEIR EXPECTATIONS.

▣ Read! Read! Read! The most helpful resources for beginning home schoolers are found in the Founder's Choice Section of Elijah Company's online catalog available at www.elijahcompany.com.

VETERAN HOME SCHOOLER?

If you've taught at home for several years, you probably have a good idea of the materials that are available and of what your children need. You may be experiencing one or more of the following:

▣ You may be tired of the teaching materials you are using and want something more suited to your family's needs. Maybe your children's interests have changed, or your focus has changed.

▣ You may find your enthusiasm and interest waning and need to renew your vision, get back in touch with the reasons you chose to home school, or just need a change.

▣   You may be wanting to move away from traditional text teaching approaches. You might even be considering creating your own curriculum that meets your family's unique needs.

▣   You may be looking for resources to round out your studies in each subject.

7

IT IS DISHEARTENING and somewhat overwhelming to consider the problems confronting us as Christian home educators. We risk misunderstanding from family, friends, and public officials. We assume the cost as well as the responsibility for making sure our children become educated. But far worse, although we long to give our children the kind of upbringing that would draw them close to the Lord, our own educations have steeped us in a man-centered agenda and equipped us with information and skills that are not necessarily in the best interests of the Kingdom of God. As Marilyn Howshall says in *A Lifestyle of Learning*:

> *Our generation was not taught how to learn and was never given a love of learning. Yet our children are trained with the same methods that failed to teach us to learn or to love learning. With only the raw material of our fragmented lives to work with, we attempt to integrate our new vision, godly desires, and goals into our old lifestyles and systems. We use the world's methods to try and produce something they were never designed to produce.*

In our own lives, as we began understanding the different influences on education, God challenged us with a host of questions: What if we look at education a different way? What if we start viewing it, not as a commodity, but as an outworking of the convictions and priorities of our family? What if we see it as part of the "equipping of the saints...for the work of service?" What if we operate under a dif-

---

BEFORE WE CAN DETERMINE OUR EDUCATIONAL PHILOSOPHY, WE NEED TO GET IN TOUCH WITH OUR FAMILY'S UNIQUE VISION AND PURPOSE.

---

ferent set of assumptions than institutional education? Assumptions like: [1] God has created our particular family unit and given us our particular children because our family has a unique, God-ordained meaning and purpose; [2] God has put (and is putting) in our hearts the convictions and values that make up our family's unique meaning and purpose; [3] These convictions and values make up the core of the kind of people we want our children to become; [4] Our education of our children reflects these convictions and values; and [5] God will stay actively involved in the process for our children's sakes.

RECOGNIZING WHO EACH CHILD WAS CREATED TO BE

Every culture has a certain ideal of what man should be like and it is this ideal that determines how youth are trained. America's ideal man is a self-actualized wage earner who contributes to the betterment of society, and our educational systems are set up to try and create this ideal. As Neil Postman says in *The End of Education*, "...public education does not serve a public." It creates a "public" that wants to "earn more, buy more, worship technology, and cling to their ethnic differences." But what is our ideal man or woman? What kind of people do we want our children to become? More to the point, what kind of people does God want our children to become?

We suggest you imagine each child's graduation from high school (or leaving home). What do you want that child to know? What skills do you want him/her to have learned? What kind of a relationship do you want to have with that child? What kind of relationship do you want the child to have with God? What attitudes? What would it take for you to be able to say, "We're done!" What would it take to look back with few regrets about how you spent the years that child was in your care? What would it take for the Lord to say, "Well done, good and faithful parents!"

God made each of our sons and daughters and created them with a life purpose. Our job as parents is to uncover this purpose and to equip each child with the skills, tools, and information to fulfill it. If we start with the end and work backwards, we have a better idea of the path to follow. If children are, as the Bible says, "arrows in the hand of a warrior," then what is the target at which we are aiming? What is the battle for which we are preparing?

There are three areas of competence that are vital to becoming strong, capable, effective, and productive adults. The three areas are relationships, skills, and information.

Recognizing who each child was created to be is an ongoing process, but there are certain attitudes and skills that are essential to succeeding in a changing world. Think about what really determines success in life. We live in a world where we can no longer count on job security, a support network of family and friends, strong spiritual ties, or education guaranteeing prosperity (or even guaranteeing a job).

What are the qualities of strong, capable, productive adults? What gives meaning and purpose to life? What are the attitudes, character qualities, and knowledge the Bible says are important to have? Each family's answer to these questions will be different, based on the family's values and convictions. We believe that God placed our children in our family (and not in yours) because our family has a unique reflection of the Kingdom of God and we are the only ones who can impart that reflection to our children. Your family's reflection will be different from ours, your picture of your children's future will be different, and therefore the way you educate your children will be different.

When we begin thinking of home education as an extension of God's purpose for our family, we realize that before we can determine our "educational philosophy," we need to get in touch with our family's unique vision and purpose. This is not something that can be done overnight, but we can begin asking ourselves questions like: "What is the purpose of our family?" "What kind of family do we want?" "What are the things that are truly important to us as a family?" "What unique interests, concerns, talents, or abilities has the Lord given us?" "What guiding principles do we find ourselves living our lives by?"

DEVELOPING AN IEP

IEP is educational jargon for Individualized Educational Plan. What this means is that a specific educational plan is developed for each child. In an institutionalized school setting, IEPs are often reserved for children with learning difficulties so that their progress can be charted in areas such as reading or math. This is not the kind of IEP we think home schoolers need. The kind of IEP we recommend is one that helps you assess your children's strengths and weaknesses in the areas of competence your family believes are important.

What areas should we use to assess the strengths and weaknesses of our children? Over the years we have concluded that there are three areas of competence that are vital to becoming strong, capable, effective, and productive adults, and that are essential to effectively fulfilling any future role our children may have. These three areas of competence are relationships, skills, and information. These competencies are in this order of importance: relationships first, skills second, and information last.

Relationships First

We believe that there are four relationships in life, and our emotional, physical, and spiritual well-being depends on how balanced we are in these four areas of relationships.

Our first and primary relationship is with God. Everyone relates to God in some form of acknowledgment or denial. Our relationship with God is crucial because it affects how we relate to everything else. How we view God and how we think He views us will be reflected in everything we do and in how we treat the other three relationships of life. Our relationship with God gives us our internal sense of what matters in life, of right and wrong, and of who we are.

Our second relationship is with self. This not only has to do with personal care of our spirit, soul, and body, but how we view ourselves, what kind of people we are, what motivates and drives us, our value and belief systems, our sense of meaning and purpose. Who we are inside is manifested in how we treat our minds, bodies, and emotions, and is a reflection of our relationship with God.

A child's personal relationship with his God is molded by his upbringing; by how his parents relate to him as an example of how the child's "real" father feels toward him. A child grows up within the sphere of his parents' beliefs in how he will "turn out." He internalizes these attitudes as being those of God, Himself.

I have spent many years watching parents interact with their children. I have come to realize that the relationship one's parents have with *their* Father is never more clearly demonstrated than when they begin raising children. Some adults have never had a revelation that "it was for freedom that Christ set us free." They raise their children as if Principles were the constant and People were the variable, rather than the other way round. They are so afraid their children will make bad choices, they don't allow them to make enough choices to learn what a bad choice costs.

This is Law. These parents are often frustrated and angry with their child and the child grows up feeling he can do little to please his parents since every act and attitude is scrutinized in light of whether or not it meets some predetermined standard. These children grow up hearing more talk about honoring parents and not being disobedient than about the sacrifice of Christ—which empowers us all to show the world how great it is to be in Him; about God's forgiveness when we sin; and about how much God believes in His own capacity to fulfill the "good work" He began when He created this child.

Our third relationship is with others. Our culture encourages us to consider people disposable, as commodities, and makes possessions and personal pleasure more important than people. But Jesus said that loving others as yourself is the second great commandment, second only to loving God.

Our fourth relationship is with created things. How we relate to time, money, work, possessions, animals, the earth, and so on.

The actual meaning of the word righteousness is "right relationship," and refers to being "rightly related" to God. We want our children to be righteous in their relationship with God, but also "rightly related" in each of the other areas of relationships.

Skills Second

When we think of all the possible skills a person could develop, the list is endless. However, if we ask ourselves, "What are the bottom line skills of life?" the list shrinks considerably. Each family's bottom line life skills will be different, but these are the skills we feel every adult should have: Relational Skills, Thinking Skills, Gender Skills, Aptitude/Interest/Gifting Skills, and Academic Skills.

Relational Skills. These are skills that enhance our relationship with God: skills like a familiarity with the Bible, the ability to use Bible study materials, a basic understanding of church history and different church doctrines, perhaps even the ability to translate the Bible from the original Greek or Hebrew. There are other spiritual skills such as an active prayer life, praise and worship, and so forth. None of these skills is essential for salvation, but each gives greater depth to our relationship with God.

There are certain skills that smooth the way for relationships with others. For example, Communication skills such as reading, writing, speaking, good body language, listening, and observing help build relationships. Good manners are also important relational skills. Character is another relational skill. Character qualities are those attitudes and actions that pave the way for better relationships with God, ourselves, others, and created things such as time, money, possessions, and work.

In addition to communication skills and character, social skills are very important. Social skills include such things as: ways of interacting with others, the ability to put other people at ease and engage them in conversation, proper ways of persuading and influencing others, knowing how to act in different social situations, strategies for resolving conflict, and so forth.

Because we expect our children to have to enter the work force at some time in their lives, we include business skills under relational skills. Why? Because much of what makes an employee valuable to a company or to a boss is not technical expertise but character qualities such as punctuality, dependability, initiative, and honesty, as well as relational skills such as working well with others, submitting to authority, and so on.

Thinking Skills. In the 1940s, British author Dorothy Sayers warned that schools were teaching children everything except how to think, and non-thinking children become adults who are easily swayed by the opinions of others. Sayers said, "the sole true end of education is simply this: to teach men how to learn for themselves; and whatever instruction fails to do this is effort spent in vain."

In the book *Endangered Minds,* author Jane Healy explains that children (and adults) today have shorter attention spans, are less able to concentrate, and are less able to absorb and analyze information than any previous generation. In short, people today do not know how to think. We believe that thinking skills are crucial life skills that prepare children to become adults who can solve whatever problems the future brings their way. Thinking skills include such skills as knowing how to learn (self-learners can pick up whatever information they need when they need it); research skills (knowing how to find what you need to know); logic (recognizing truth and fallacy); and organizational skills (being able to prioritize, to manage time, money, and surroundings, getting the important things done, etc.). Thinking skills also include understanding world views, and having the doctrinal training to be able to give "a reason for the hope within you."

Gender Skills. As we prepare our sons for adulthood, we have tried to determine which skills will make them better men, husbands, and fathers. There are many traditionally masculine skills that are very helpful for husbands to know such as basic auto mechanics, how to repair simple machines, building and woodworking skills, home maintenance, perhaps land management and how to raise food or livestock. These skills will not only come in handy when our boys are adults, but they also give a sense of manliness which is a component of true masculinity. There are other skills that may seem superficial, but can have a real bearing on manliness in our culture: skills like the ability to play a sport well enough to take part in a pick-up game of basketball or football, or to play golf, or at least the ability to discuss a sport intelligently. These are the things men in our culture do when they get together, so it may be wise for our sons to have some understanding of them.

In the same way, there are certain skills that make being a woman, wife and mother more satisfying such as preparing nourishing meals, home management, interior decorating, child care, sewing, and so forth.

Aptitude/Interest/Gifting Skills. God has made each of our children with unique aptitudes, interests, and gifts. We have to assume that these innate abilities are part of God's plan for each child and somehow fit into the life purpose God has for him or her. For example, our son Blake has an artistic bent. He has noticed colors and textures and tried to draw things since he was very young. Our son James is gifted with an understanding of people and also has a desire to sing and act. Seth is totally different from James and Blake. He understands machines and how they work. As we have recognized these aptitudes, interests, and giftings, we have encouraged them by providing opportunities to develop them. In every way we can, we "feed" the interests, develop the aptitudes, and encourage the giftings.

Academic Skills. Reading, writing, and math are crucial life skills. All of the other subjects fall under the category of Information.

The best way to determine our childrens' emotional, physical and intellectual needs is to think about the roles each is likely to have as an adult (see below).

Information Last

Information is our lowest priority, ranking below relationships and skills, even though diplomas, degrees, and SAT scores hinge on the accumulation of vast amounts of information. There is no question that the 3-Rs (reading, writing, and arithmetic) are foundational to all further learning, so they must be mastered. However, we believe that once our children are rightly related to God, self, others, and created things and once they acquire the life skills mentioned above, they can pick up any other information they need when it becomes useful or when it is required (such as for admission to a certain college program).

FUTURE RESPONSIBILITIES

So far, we have encouraged you to give thought to your family's unique vision and purpose and to try and determine the individual interests, concerns, talents, or abilities the Lord has given your children. The next step is to consider the responsibilities each child is likely to have as an adult.

Adult life consists of three basic arenas: [1] Public (situations, relationships, and interactions outside of our immediate family), [2] Family (interactions with those related to us), and [3] Private (our inner spiritual, emotional, and mental life). Each of these arenas has its own set of demands and responsibilities.

We can think of these adult arenas in terms of "roles." Once we know each child's probable future roles, we can concentrate on the relationships, skills and information that would be most helpful in assuming the responsibilities required by each role. Here are adult roles your children are likely to have:

- Child of God role (includes life purpose, calling, ministry)
- Member of the Body of Christ role (includes spiritual giftings)
- Family Member role (as daughter, son, cousin, uncle, aunt, grandchild, etc.)
- Spouse role (as husband or wife)
- Parent role (as father or mother)
- Friend role
- Worker role (as employer or employee)
- Community Member role (member of organizations, sports teams, etc.)

When we look at our children's futures in terms of the roles they may play, it helps us focus on the relationships, skills, and information they should acquire. For example, if we believe our sons will become fathers one day, it would be to their advantage to learn about fatherhood and child rearing. If we believe our daughters will someday be employed, we can help them learn skills consistent with their God-given abilities that will be useful to them as adults. The more specific we can be about our children's future roles, the easier it becomes to identify what we want to impart to them.

Authors Linda and Richard Eyre in *Teaching Your Children Responsibility* explain that responsibility means "to become mature in the sense of being responsible to family, to self, to society. It means being responsible for all aspects of our lives and our situations; for our talents, for our potential, for our feelings, for our thoughts, for our actions, for our freedom. Responsibility is not the result of maturity, but the cause of it—and a major responsibility of parents is to teach responsibility."

Robert Barnes, in *Ready for Responsibility*, says:

> *If there is no plan, no philosophy of life, there can be nothing but conflict between the three primary arenas of*

life...It's the parents' job to raise a marriageable child. And most important, it's the parents' job to raise children who are able to be used by God to fulfill God's purpose for each child when that child reaches adulthood. It's the parents' job to establish a plan that will train a child in the skills he or she will need to be a responsible adult.

BACK TO THE IEP

Once you have given some thought to your family's mission and purpose, to each child's future public, personal, and family life, and to the individual interests, concerns, talents, or abilities the Lord has given your children, you are in a position to think about the relationships, life skills, and academics you feel are appropriate for each child. This doesn't have to be intense or complicated, just begin by jotting down the areas that are important to your family. In the Real Needs Framework at right, we have listed the areas that are important to us, but that doesn't mean what we consider important needs to show up on your list. You want to develop a list that is specific to your family's mission and purpose.

As you can see, the three areas on our list are interrelated. For example, under Relationships we have "With Others," under Life Skills we have "Social Skills," and under Information we have "Reading, Writing, and Speaking." The Relationships column would mainly deal with developing biblical perspectives and attitudes toward relationships with others. The "Social Skills" in the Life Skills column would have more to do with specific ways of relating to others such as developing conversational skills, being sensitive to the moods of others, learning proper ways to persuade and influence, demonstrating poise and tasteful fashion sense, etc. However, many of these social skills are dependent on mastering the Information involved in using proper grammar when speaking and writing, having the foundational knowledge to have something worth sharing with someone else, and so forth.

When you know the categories of Relationships, Skills, and Information that are important to you, then you can begin choosing specific activities or programs that develop them in each child, according to the child's natural abilities and level of maturity. The only pitfalls to looking at the "big picture" is that we often want to accomplish too much too fast, so we need a sense of what is developmentally appropriate for our children as well as a sense of how each learns best. As a general rule, you would focus on relationships, discipline, good work habits, basic skills, and foundational academics (reading, writing, and arithmetic) with younger children.

When the children reach upper elementary ages their interests, talents, or giftings will become more pronounced and can be pursued more earnestly; they will be capable of more responsibility for learning the skills on your Life Skills list; and their academic studies can be more in-depth. They also will have developed problem-solving skills that allow them to expand their courses of study into areas that are more self-directed.

By the high school level, parents usually have a feel for whether their children should go to college, attend a trade school, or simply enter the job market; so the high school years can be a time of mastering independent living skills and pursuing academics to the intensity required by their future plans. At this stage, children who have had a broad academic foundation and who have been allowed to pursue their interests in-depth should be able to teach themselves with a minimum of oversight from you.

8

JUST AS CHRISTENDOM IS comprised of many diverse groups, each having a unique doctrinal emphasis, Christian homeschoolers are a diverse people. The Department of Education estimates there are between one and two million home schooling families in the United States, most of whom are teaching their children out of a religious conviction.

As we have traveled to various book fairs throughout the country, we have been able to interact with homeschoolers holding differing doctrinal positions, and those positions are reflected in the lifestyles the families lead as well as in the teaching materials they choose. At the risk of reducing homeschoolers to stereotypes or of misrepresenting their views, we would like to share the main convictions/lifestyles we have seen in the home schooling movement: the "currents" within the "river." Our groupings are not rigid, because there is a broad spectrum of beliefs within each group and the groups tend to overlap.

COMMON FAMILY EMPHASES

From our vantage point these are the four main emphases among Christian home schooling families:

Families concerned with social action.

Many home educators long to see our government reflect Christian principles and therefore are preparing their children to become the intellectual, social, and spiritual leaders of tomorrow. These families tend to be involved in a broad spectrum of social concerns. They may be active in the Pro-Life movement or in organizations that address legislative and/or social change. Their focus may be on the study of America's Christian history and restoring truths that are omitted by secular historians. They want their children prepared to influence the world and therefore want them to understand world views and current events and to be informed about the problems facing America. The study of history and government, particularly the study of America's Christian heritage, is strongly encouraged. These families tend to share Calvinist or Reconstructionist theology.

Families desiring a more simple, self-reliant lifestyle.

A growing number of home schooling families tend to be very ecologically aware, and are interested in cooking more naturally and nutritiously, alternative medicines, large families, breast-feeding, home birth, midwifery, home businesses, building their own homes, raising their own food, homesteading, survival skills, and becoming as self-sufficient as possible. Some of these families have adopted lifestyles similar to the Amish and seek to protect their children from many of the issues facing the outside world. Others are more socially active, but greatly limit outside influences over their children. Preferred teaching materials reinforce biblical order in the home, simplicity of life-style, and the values of hard work and resourcefulness.

Families concerned with restoration of the family and of the Church.

The primary focus of many teaching families is to build strong, capable men who can lead their families well; to develop virtuous women who can succeed as wives and mothers; to create a family unit that nourishes Christian character in the children; and to build churches that are family-based in their orientation and ministry. These fami-

---

REAL BOOKS EDUCATE, SCHOOL BOOKS SCHOOL.

John Taylor Gatto

---

lies believe that because the church is made up of family units, it can be no purer nor stronger than its members, so the restoration of the Christian family is critical to the restoration of the Church to her rightful place of leadership and power. Family-based churches are built on the godly family units of which they are composed and strive to include the whole family in the various facets of church life. Families with this focus tend to choose teaching materials that reinforce traditional family roles and emphasize separation from the world. Many lean toward Pietist theology.

Families whose children need special care.
Some of these may be families who have children with handicaps or children who need special care. The vast majority of this group, however, is made up of families who have had disappointing or disturbing encounters with the public school system and no longer want their children exposed to its negative influences. These families tend to take one of two paths: either they choose a prepackaged traditional curriculum and reproduce what their children were doing in the public school classroom, or they reject classroom-style learning entirely and become "unschoolers."

COMMON EDUCATIONAL PHILOSOPHIES

There are four educational philosophies influencing education today. Think of these philosophies as the underlying assumptions about what comprises an education and what the teaching materials should cover in a course of study. All of the common teaching approaches available to home educators contain elements of these four educational philosophies.

Essentialism assumes that there is a core body of knowledge that must be mastered in order for a person to be considered "educated." It focuses on the "essentials" and is subject oriented. Essentialism could be summed up in this phrase: "Information is the key to a good education."

Perennialism is more "idea" oriented, and considers education to consist of becoming acquainted with the great writing and thinking throughout history. To perennialists, "understanding is the key to a good education."

Progressivism seeks to make education practical and applicable to the needs of students and society. It assumes that making knowledge and skills meaningful are the keys to a good education.

Existentialism stresses "authenticity" the commitment to finding true being. To the existentialist, discovering one's own meaning and purpose in life is the key to a good education.

COMMON TEACHING APPROACHES

Your family emphases and your educational philosophy will tend to influence your teaching approach. Although there are many variations on the teaching approaches listed here, we've found these groupings to be a helpful framework for understanding the whole spectrum of teaching. We've divided them into the following two main curriculum teaching groups: Traditional (Textbook and Workbook, or "Worktext" categories) and Non-Textbook (with Classical, Unit Studies, Living Books, Principal, Unschooling and Mixed categories).

The Traditional Approach

In the Traditional Approach, graded textbooks or workbooks follow a scope and sequence that covers each subject in 180 daily increments over a span of 12 years. Teacher's manuals, tests, and record keeping materials are usually available that correspond to each of the texts. Textbook curricula assume you will run your home school like an institutional school.

Worktext programs present textbooks in consumable workbook format. The student learns his lesson, is given assignments, and is tested all in the workbook. The worktexts include tests or checkpoints to ensure that the material in each section is mastered before the student moves on to the next. Worktexts also allow more independent study and require minimal teacher preparation time and supervision. Video programs are also available that are actual classrooms on video. The child follows along with the video as if he or she were attending an actual classroom, and uses the accompanying textbooks or workbooks. Traditional curricula are also available on computer. Many satellite schools and well as universities now offer computer courses on CD or through the internet.

Most of the textbook programs used in private Christian schools are available to homeschoolers. They each share a distinct doctrinal perspective, and usually contain strong elements of essentialism.

QUESTIONS TO ASK

Some questions to ask yourself before trying the traditional, textbook approach are listed below. Yes answers indicate this approach may work for you and your child:

- Did my child perform well in a school classroom?
- Does my child like to complete assignments and to have

defined goals?

- ▣ Is my child academically oriented?
- ▣ Will my child complete assigned tasks with a minimum of prodding from me?
- ▣ Am I the kind of person who will follow through with the lesson plans and pace of the course of instruction?

Some additional questions to ask before using the workbook approach with your child:

- ▣ Does my child read well and have good reading comprehension skills?
- ▣ Can my child work well independently?
- ▣ Can my child learn without a lot of variety in teaching materials?

STRENGTHS OF THE TEXTBOOK/WORKBOOK APPROACH

- ▣ Everything is laid out for ease of use
- ▣ Follows a standardized scope and sequence
- ▣ Has definite milestones of accomplishment
- ▣ Testing and assigning grades is easy to do

WEAKNESSES OF THE TEXTBOOK/WORKBOOK APPROACH

- ▣ Is geared to the "generic" child. Does not take into account individual learning styles, strengths and weaknesses, or interests
- ▣ Assumes that there is a body of information that comprises an education and that this information can be broken down into daily increments
- ▣ Treats children's minds like containers to fill with information
- ▣ Focuses on transmitting information through artificial learning experiences
- ▣ Is teacher-directed and chalkboard oriented

- ☐ Different aged students study different materials
- ☐ Expensive when teaching multiple children
- ☐ Discourages original, independent thinking
- ☐ Has a high "burn out" rate

Non-Textbook Approaches

Although there are a number of excellent textbook and worktext programs available, many home educators object to the fact that textbooks are teacher-directed, chalkboard-oriented, and seldom take into account different teaching approaches or the different ways children receive and process information.

John Gatto says, "Real books educate. School books school." With textbooks, parents may feel they are "bringing the classroom home" instead of educating their children in a way that is uniquely home-based. These parents have found alternative teaching approaches that allow them to tailor their home schooling to their family's particular needs. The following is a brief explanation of the five most common non-textbook teaching approaches:

The *Classical Approach* is derived from successful courses of study throughout history and recently revived through the writings of Dorothy Sayers.

The *Principle Approach* is based on the premise that our nation is a unique and vital link in the westward chain of Christianity.

The *Living Books and Life Experiences Approach* of Charlotte Mason treats children as persons, not as containers to be filled with information.

The *Unit Study Approach* integrates several subject areas around a common theme.

The *Unschooling Approach* assumes that children are natural learners and gives them resources to do so.

The Classical Approach

The Classical Approach to education has produced great minds throughout history, and has strong elements of perennialism. The modern proponent of the Classical Approach was British writer and medieval scholar Dorothy Sayers. As the Nazis rose to power in the 1930s, Sayers warned that schools were teaching children everything except how to think. Because young adults could no longer think for themselves, Sayers felt they could be easily influenced by tyrants. To remedy this, Sayers proposed reinstating the classical form of education used in the Middle Ages.

In the Classical Approach, children under age 18 are taught tools of learning collectively known as The Trivium. The Trivium has three parts, each part corresponding to a childhood developmental stage.

The first stage of the Trivium, the Grammar Stage, covers early elementary ages and focuses on reading, writing, and spelling; the study of Latin; and developing observation, listening and memorization skills. The goal of this stage is to develop a general framework of knowledge and to acquire basic language arts and math skills.

At approximately middle school age, children begin to demonstrate independent or abstract thought (usually by becoming argumentative or opinionated). This signals the beginning of the Dialectic Stage in which the child's tendency to argue is molded and shaped by teaching logical discussion, debate, and how to draw correct conclusions and support them with facts. The goal of this stage is to equip the child with language and thinking skills capable of detecting fallacies in an argument. Latin study is continued, with the possible addition of Greek and Hebrew. The student reads essays, arguments and criticisms instead of literature as in the Grammar Stage. History study leans toward interpreting events. Higher math and theology begin.

The final phase of the Trivium, the Rhetoric Stage, seeks to produce a student who can use language, both written and spoken, eloquently and persuasively. Students are usually ready for this stage by age 15.

QUESTIONS TO ASK

Here are some questions to ask yourself before trying the classical approach with your child:

- Does my family like to read good literature?
- Are my children intellectually oriented and comfortable with a rigorous academic program?
- Am I a learner? Am I comfortable learning alongside my children so I can teach them things I never studied?
- Do I like to study ideas that have influenced civilization?

STRENGTHS OF THE CLASSICAL APPROACH

- Is tailored to stages of mental development
- Teaches thinking skills & verbal/written expression
- Creates self-learners
- Has produced great minds throughout history

WEAKNESSES OF THE CLASSICAL APPROACH

- Very little prepared curriculum available
- Requires a scholarly teacher and student
- May overemphasize ancient disciplines and classics

The Unit Study Approach

A Unit Study takes a theme or topic (a unit of study) and delves into it deeply over a period of time, integrating language arts, science, social studies, math, and fine arts as they apply. Instead of studying eight or ten separate, unrelated subjects, all subjects are blended together and studied around a common theme or project. For example, a unit study on birds could include reading and writing about birds and about famous ornithologists (language arts), studying the parts, functions, and life cycles of birds and perhaps even the aerodynamics of flight (science and math), determining the migration paths, habitats, and ecological/sociological impact of birds (social studies), sketching familiar birds (art), building bird houses or feeders ("hands on" activities) and so forth.

Several fine prepared unit study curricula are available, but it is easy to prepare your own unit studies around areas of interest. History is the logical core curriculum to build ongoing unit studies around. History provides a framework for all the other subjects because it follows a progression and covers every other subject (except possibly math), like art, music, science, literature, and so on.

QUESTIONS TO ASK

Here are some questions to ask yourself before trying unit studies with your children:

- Am I a creative person?
- Do I like trying to make everything interesting and fun?
- Do my children have a variety of interests and learning styles?
- Can I live with the fact that there may be "gaps" in my children's education?
- Do I have the time and energy to be the driving, creative force behind the development of units?

STRENGTHS OF THE UNIT STUDY APPROACH

- All ages can learn together
- Children can delve as deeply or as lightly into a subject as they like

- The family's interests can be pursued
- Students get the whole picture
- Curiosity and independent thinking are generated
- Intense study of one topic is the more natural way to learn
- Knowledge is interrelated so is learned easily and remembered longer
- Unit studies are fairly easy to create

WEAKNESSES OF THE UNIT STUDY APPROACH
- It is easy to leave educational "gaps"
- Hard to assess the level of learning occurring
- Record keeping may be difficult
- Prepared unit study curricula are expensive
- Do-it-yourself unit studies require planning
- Too many activity-oriented unit studies may cause burn-out of teacher and student
- Subjects that are hard to integrate into the unit may be neglected

The Living Books Approach

The Living Books Approach is based on the writings of Charlotte Mason, a turn-of-the-century British educator. Miss Mason was appalled by several tendencies she noticed in modern education: [1] the tendency to treat children as containers to be filled with predigested information instead of as human beings; [2] the tendency to break down knowledge into thousands of isolated bits of information to be fed into "container" children; and [3] the tendency to engineer artificial learning experiences. She believed in respecting children as persons, in involving them in real-life situations, and in allowing them to read really good books instead of what she called "twaddle" worthless, inferior teaching material. She considered education a failure when it produced children able to "do harder sums and read harder books" who lacked "moral and intellectual power." Children were to be taught good habits, to be involved in a broad spectrum of real-life situations, and given ample time to play, reflect, and create.

Mason's approach to academics was to teach basic reading, writing, and math skills, then expose children to the best sources of knowledge for all other subjects. This meant giving children experiences like nature walks, observing and collecting wildlife; visiting art museums; and reading real books with "living ideas." She called such books "living books" because they made the subject "come alive" unlike textbooks that tend to be dry and dull and assume the reader cannot think for him/herself.

QUESTIONS TO ASK

Here are some questions to ask yourself before trying the Charlotte Mason method:

- Does our family love to read, both alone and together through reading aloud?
- Do we love to go to the library?
- Am I comfortable with a "free-form" approach to learning?
- Will I follow through with teaching my children good habits and character qualities?
- Do I trust my children to learn on their own?
- Will I follow through with exposing my children firsthand to nature and to great art?

STRENGTHS OF THE LIVING BOOKS APPROACH

- Treats children as active participants in the learning process
- Exposes children to real objects and books instead of interactions with distilled information

- Encourages curiosity, creative thinking, and a love of learning
- Eliminates meaningless tasks, busywork
- Developmentally appropriate
- Stresses formation of good character and habits

WEAKNESSES OF THE LIVING BOOKS APPROACH

- Tends to be very child centered
- Very little prepared curriculum
- May neglect higher level studies because of its emphasis on art, literature, and nature study
- May become too eclectic

The Principle Approach

The Principle Approach is an effort to restore to American Christians three vital concepts: the knowledge of our Christian history; an understanding of our role in the spread of Christianity; and the ability to live according to the Biblical principles upon which our country was founded. The Principle Approach is a way of living life, not just a way of educating children. Developers of the Principle Approach rediscovered seven Biblical principles upon which our country was founded and by which many of the founding fathers were educated.

The seven principles are :

[1] Individuality (God has created distinct differences in people, nations, etc.)

[2] Self Government (Government starts in the heart of man.)

[3] Christian Character

[4] Conscience is the Most Sacred of Property

[5] The Christian Form of Government

[6] How the Seed of Local Self Government is Planted

[7] The Christian Principle of American Political Union.

Four emphases are unique to this educational approach. First, there is a recognition of God's Hand (Providence) in history. Second, there is the understanding that God has ordained three governmental institutions (the home, the church, and civil government) through which He unfolds His purposes and manifests Christ on this earth. Third, each Christian is responsible for extending God's government. Fourth, the student assumes responsibility for learning and for applying knowledge to his own life.

The Principle Approach may be applied to the study of any subject with the use of notebooks to record "the 4 R's" (Researching God's Word; Reasoning from the researched Biblical truths/ principles; Relating the truths and principles discovered to the subject and the student's character; and Recording the individual application of the Biblical principles to the subject and the student).

QUESTIONS TO ASK

Here are some questions to ask before trying the Principle Approach:

- ▣ Do I have a real concern for the application of Christian principles to my family and my nation?
- ▣ Will my child assume responsibility for a great deal of learning on his/her own?
- ▣ Does my child like to express him or herself through writing?
- ▣ Am I willing to undertake extensive biblical research and teaching preparation?

STRENGTHS OF THE PRINCIPLE APPROACH

- ▣ Students learn to think "governmentally"
- ▣ Students become self-learners

- ▣ Students learn to apply biblical principles to the whole of life
- ▣ Students create their own "textbooks"

WEAKNESSES OF THE PRINCIPLE APPROACH

- ▣ May present a narrow view of life and of history
- ▣ Focuses mainly on American history
- ▣ Requires a great deal of teacher preparation
- ▣ Prepared curriculum available in few subjects
- ▣ Extremely literal approach to Scripture

The Unschooling Approach

The Unschooling Approach is defined by John Holt, a 20th century American educator who concluded that children have an innate desire to learn and a curiosity that drives them to learn what they need to know when they need to know it. Holt believed that both desire and curiosity are destroyed by the usual methods of teaching. In his book *Teach Your Own*, Holt wrote: "What children need is not new and better curricula but access to more and more of the real world; plenty of time and space to think over their experiences, and to use nd play to make meaning out of them; and advice, road maps, guidebooks, to make it easier for them to get where they want to go (not where we think they ought to go), and to find out what they want to find out."

On the other hand, unschooling refers to any less structured learning approach that allows children to pursue their own interests with parental support and guidance. The child is surrounded by a rich environment of books, learning resources, and adults who model a lifestyle of learning and are willing to interact with him. Formal academics are pursued when the need arises. Christians who favor less structured schooling, but with definite goals, prefer to be called "relaxed home educators," not unschoolers.

QUESTIONS TO ASK

Some questions to ask before trying the Unschooling Approach:

- Am I comfortable with few pre-set goals and little structure?
- Do my children have strong interests in particular areas?
- Does my family have a lot of natural curiosity and love learning?

STRENGTHS OF THE UNSCHOOLING APPROACH

- Takes little planning
- Captures the childs "teachable moments"
- Children have access to the real world, plenty of time and space to figure things out on their own
- Children are less likely to become academically frustrated or "burned out"
- Children can delve into a subject as deeply or as shallowly as they desire
- Provides a discipleship model of learning
- Creates self-learners with a love of learning

WEAKNESSES OF THE UNSCHOOLING APPROACH

- May neglect some subjects
- Hard to assess level of learning
- Lacks the security of a clearly laid out program
- Is extremely child-centered
- Difficult to explain to others
- May be overly optimistic about what children will accomplish on their own

The Mixed Approach

Many homeschoolers use a blend of the different approaches. For example, they may use traditional math and science textbooks, but build unit studies around historical periods that include language arts, music, art, and philosophy, and then choose a computer program to teach typing.

9

THE NINETEENTH CENTURY IRISH POET, W.B. Yeats once said, "Education is not the filling of a bucket, but the lighting of a fire." As Christian parents who want to "light fires" in the hearts and minds of our children, we can take the best of all of the teaching approaches and the best of the learning theory and allow God to design our courses of study.

Parents with several school-aged children often try a modified unit study approach with all children studying the same general period of history, the same area of science, and the same language arts skills, just at different levels of intensity and with different teaching materials. One child may do well with workbooks, one may need more "hands-on," and another may thrive just by reading books about the historical period or area of scientific inquiry. The important things are that the children are learning and Mom or Dad are not pulling out their hair trying to keep up with four or more different children taking six or more different subjects.

When we are sensitive to our children's needs and to the leading of the Holy Spirit we may find that what worked well one year doesn't work the next or what frustrated a child in the past suddenly has become easy. Sometimes we forget that children change, their needs change, their interests change, and their level of skill changes. Our challenge is to be flexible, adjusting our course as we go so that we maximize our children's learning potentials and keep that "fire" alive.

The beauty of home schooling is that we can pick and choose, selecting teaching materials and products that have the most promise for our situation and budget. We can discard unworkable materials at any time. We can integrate any or all of the teaching approaches we like as we seek the most productive means of educating our children.

The teaching environment is an important factor in learning. Children learn best in a positive, affirming atmosphere with enjoyable surroundings where they are comfortable physically and emotionally. Many learning specialists are discovering that children are often labeled "learning disabled" when actually the teaching method or environment frustrates their ability to learn.

USING LEARNING THEORY BENEFICIALLY
Try and create a comfortable, physically and emotionally affirming, relaxed learning environment.

- Look for and eliminate destructive hidden messages and background thoughts (examples: expectations that are either too high or too low, manipulating methods, favoritism, dislike of the subject, negative terms of speech, comparisons between children, etc.).

- Set up the physical surroundings for the comfort of the child. (Right temperature, adequate lighting, minimal distractions, comfortable reading area, etc.)

Use every opportunity for:

- Visual aids such as actual objects or replicas, drawings, photos, diagrams, charts, colors, videotapes.

☐ Auditory aids such as sounds, music, poetry and poetic language, discussion, speaking while doing, recitation, singing, storytelling, reading aloud, reading into a tape recorder.

OUR CHALLENGE IS TO BE FLEXIBLE, ADJUSTING OUR COURSE AS WE GO SO THAT WE MAXIMIZE OUR CHILDREN'S LEARNING POTENTIAL AND KEEP THAT "FIRE" ALIVE.

☐ Kinesthetic aids such as manipulatives, working with clay, handling models, drama, dance, acting out, lapping, pounding, or passing a ball back and forth while reciting, playing , human sculptures.

☐ Discussion through question and answer, intensive listening, and conversation.

☐ Lots of print exposure through reading and writing.

☐ Using the imagination through visualizing shapes or processes; picturing a condition, person, or situation in the mind; imagining being part of the situation.

☐ Direct experience such as nature walks, field trips, lab experiments, building models, seeing and working with real things.

☐ "Bridging" by relating new information to something already known, using metaphors, parables, analogies.

☐ Synthesizing by categorizing, classifying, analyzing, reasoning through the logical basis of the subject, finding the core concept.

☐ Time for reflection, time for being listened to, time for thinking.

Included in each area of study should be:

- ▣ *Focusing:* discussing what the activity is about, what will be done, and the results expected; giving an overview of what will be covered; introducing new vocabulary
- ▣ *Application:* feedback, summarizing, applying the concept
- ▣ *Ritual:* an ongoing structure or schedule

10

CHOOSING TEACHING MATERIALS CAN be an overwhelming task because there are so many excellent products available and each one claims to be superior to all others. Many veteran home schoolers suggest that you stick to a "prepackaged" traditional curriculum for the first year or so. Others encourage new home schoolers to consider correspondence schools. We do not completely agree with these recommendations, because for many it seems to perpetuate a mentality of home schooling as being "school at home" instead of an exciting lifestyle of learning. We know that it takes some experience to determine which materials are best suited to your teaching style and your children's needs, but we are also convinced that the Lord can lead concerned parents to the teaching materials and methods that work best for their family. Here are some suggestions concerning choosing curricula:

RULE 1 | INVEST IN YOURSELF FIRST.
Like it or not, you are the glue that will hold this home schooling endeavor together, so you need to develop a strategy for staying sane and on top of it all (even if it means scheduling a nap every

afternoon). You wouldn't dream of trying to build a house without a plan, the right materials, and the necessary tools. Home schooling is like building a house: You need to determine your plan, gather your materials, and be sure you have the right tools for the job. Take some time to read, to look around, to compare. Invest in some of the "tools of the trade" like the everyone's favorite books on homeschooling. Begin rearranging your house so it will accommodate study without becoming too cluttered or stressful. Think through what you will do with infants and toddlers during school times; how you will handle meals, house cleaning, and laundry; and how you will deal with the other changes schooling at home brings. Don't feel guilty about spending money on yourself. After all, if you were a professional teacher, you (or your parents) would have spent tens of thousands of dollars getting you ready to stand before a classroom of children. So think in terms of what will make you more confident and able to create a learning environment for your household. What will smooth your way mentally, emotionally, physically, and spiritually?

RULE 2 | CONSIDER YOUR SITUATION.

A farm family will have many opportunities for "hands on" learning in the areas of math, science, economics, etc. A city family has access to museums, libraries, cultural events, and more support group activities. You can make the most of the real life learning opportunities God gives you, perhaps never needing textbooks and teaching materials in certain subject areas. We once had a missionary call us bemoaning the fact that she lived in a large foreign city and her children weren't able to do much nature study. She completely overlooked all the wonderful opportunities her children had to learn foreign languages, history, and geography, and to interact with other cultures. So, look around. God may have already arranged a learning environment for you that is better than a classroom.

RULE 3 | CHOOSE MATERIALS THAT COMPLIMENT THE LEARNER.
Textbooks developed for classroom use tend to be "teacher directed" and chalkboard oriented, seldom taking into account children's interests or of the different ways children perceive and process information. Each student has a style in which he learns best. Different children have different learning strengths and weaknesses that the perceptive parent will take into account when choosing teaching materials. For example, visual learners may do well with workbooks, while auditory learners need songs or spoken instruction and kinesthetic learners need to manipulate objects.

YOU WILL SOON DISCOVER THAT OFTEN IT IS YOU, NOT YOUR CHILDREN, WHO ARE BEING EDUCATED. SO LOOSEN UP AND ACCEPT THE FACT THAT SOME OF WHAT YOU BUY WILL BE A TOTAL WASTE OF TIME, ENERGY, AND MONEY.

RULE 4 | IF YOU DON'T LIKE THE MATERIAL, YOU WILL RESIST USING IT NO MATTER HOW GOOD IT IS.
All teaching materials have a bias, not just in the subject matter, but also in the way the subject matter is presented. Every teaching parent, whether he or she recognizes it or not, has an educational philosophy, some set of values and beliefs about what and how children should be taught. Sometimes we will have an unexplained inner resistance to certain teaching materials. It could be that this inner resistance arises from a conflict between our educational philosophy and that of the

teaching material. Trust the Holy Spirit and choose from your spirit as well as from your head. No matter how much your friends rave about a particular product, don't buy it if you don't really like it yourself. A key question to ask is: "Does just looking at this curriculum make me feel tired or pressured?"

RULE 5 | AVOID PROGRAMS THAT REQUIRE A GREAT DEAL OF TEACHER PREPARATION.

Unless you are a researcher-type or high-energy person, you will be frustrated by programs with detailed teacher's manuals to wade through, supplemental books or seminars that are necessary to fully utilize the program, or lots of activities to prepare beforehand.

RULE 6 | EXPECT TO WASTE TIME, ENERGY, AND ESPECIALLY MONEY.

You will soon discover that often it is you, not your children, who are being educated. So loosen up and accept the fact that some of what you buy will be a total waste of time, energy, and money. This is all a part of learning what works for you and for your children. Consider it payment of your tuition in the University for Home Educating Parents.

RULE 7 | BE AWARE THAT THERE ARE VARIOUS SCHOOLS OF THOUGHT CONCERNING THE TEACHING OF ANY SUBJECT.

Some examples: In math there are programs that are primarily problem solving with manipulatives and programs that are primarily problem solving on paper. In reading there are programs that focus on learning phonics before learning to read, programs that focus on learning the rules while learning to read, and programs that focus on just learning to read and letting the rules come later. Each school of thought has produced excellent mathematicians, readers, and spellers, but sometimes products will be advertised as better than the rest because they follow a particular school of thought.

RULE 8 | REALIZE THAT THERE IS NO PERFECT CURRICULUM.

What works with one child won't necessarily work with another. What worked one year may not necessarily work the next. Your family's needs and interests will change. Buy materials that meet present needs. Mold the curriculum to the child, not the child to the curriculum. Also, be aware that not all books in a series are equally as good. For example, the fourth grade level of a particular program may be excellent, but this does not mean the other levels are.

RULE 9 | GOD GAVE YOU YOUR SPECIFIC CHILDREN BECAUSE THERE IS SOMETHING IN YOU THAT HE WANTS IMPARTED TO THEM.

Teaching materials are only tools to help you impart yourself to (discipile) your children. You can trust the Lord to lead you to those materials that will help you best disciple each child.

RULE 10 | REMEMBER THAT TEACHING MATERIALS ARE OFTEN THE LEAST IMPORTANT ELEMENTS OF YOUR HOME SCHOOL.

Books are easy to discard if they don't work for you, but attitudes and destructive family dynamics are not. Five major reasons families fail at home education are: (1) they lack the personal conviction to persevere through the difficult times; (2) the father is not involved; (3) the children are undisciplined and resist parental instruction; (4) the parents cannot handle the added responsibilities; and (5) the family has unrealistic expectations. The best teaching materials in the world are going to take a back seat to the attitudes and family dynamics in your household.

II

THERE ARE TWO KINDS of knowledge. One is represented by "the tree of the knowledge of good and evil." This type of knowledge is centered around man determining his own values, ethics, and aspirations, his own standards by which he evaluates life. He decides for himself what is "good" and what is "evil" apart from a relationship with God. This knowledge is a "knowing" about things based on their worth to man.

The Bible warns that this type of "knowing" can seem impressive, but results in chaos and death. God-centered knowledge, however, is a knowing about things from God's perspective. The Bible says: "the fear of the Lord is the beginning of wisdom and the knowledge of the holy is understanding." This means that to truly understand something, man has to see it as God sees it, out of a relationship with Him. In other words, we have to "know" Him to have understanding.

Jesus was the model child, and He only did what He saw the Father do and only said what He heard the Father say. His life was lived out of His relationship with God. It wasn't a life of rules and "dos" and "don'ts," in fact, he scolded the Pharisees for making a system of rules out of what should be a relationship. We've found ourselves so saturated with non-relational knowledge that it has been a long journey from rule-based religion to a relationship with God. This doesn't mean that we've thrown out the rules. It simply means that the rules are no longer the issue, the relationship is. Applying the rules apart from the relationship misses the point.

As we have tried to find "the ancient path" in educating our children (see Jeremiah 6:16), we have concluded that education is not as much the mastering of skills and information as it is the development of healthy relationships. We want our children to be "rightly related" to God; to themselves (personal care of their spirit, soul, and body); to others; and to created things (nature, time, money, possessions, knowledge, etc.). Academic knowledge, facts, and skills assume their proper places as they contribute to healthy relationships in each of these areas.

We also have concluded that God's "good way" of teaching is relational. We try to disciple our children so that, as much as possible, they learn to do things as they do them with us "when we sit at home, when we walk along the road, when we lie down, and when we get up."

12

CREATING A LEARNING ENVIRONMENT

WE LIVE AT AN ELEVATION of two thousand feet on wooded property with thin, acidic soil. Our winters can be fairly severe. But we've always wanted an English cottage-type flower garden. We would be foolish to think we would get good growth from tender, alkaline loving plants that need full sun. If we want to grow a cottage garden filled with sun-loving perennials (our favorites), we have to create the right environment for them to thrive. This means clearing a patch of woods, fortifying the soil and changing its pH, and using a lot of mulch to protect the plants in the winter.

Think of your home as a garden spot and your children as plants (in fact, that is the picture the Bible uses). Does where you live nurture the kind of growth you are looking for in your children? Does your lifestyle? Does the layout of your house? Does the way your house is organized? Does everything (where you live, your lifestyle, how you spend your time, how you organize, and so forth) work together to nurture the relationships, skills, and knowledge you are trying to develop in your children's lives?

The definition of context is "the setting, surroundings, or circumstances that give true or exact meaning." The word "context" comes

79

from a Latin word that means to weave or knit together into a whole. What setting, surroundings, or circumstances would give "true or exact meaning" to your children's lives? What setting, surroundings, or circumstances would weave or knit together your family and produce "whole" people?

For example, when our children were small we lived in apartments. There were certain masculine skills we wanted our boys to acquire and certain areas of physical labor we wanted them to be involved in that were not required by apartment life. We began talking about a context that would provide them with hard work and with opportunities to practice traditionally masculine skills such as construction, working with land and machinery, and working with livestock. So for years we prayed, planned, and dreamed. When the boys were 8, 6, and 3 we rented a small farm. Living there allowed us to crystallize in our thinking what we did and did not want, when we had property of our own.

Some time ago we finally realized our dream and bought our own land. Since that time we have built a barn, sheds, and fences; cleared land; learned how to use a tractor (and scraper and bush hog); planted an orchard; and raised a few collies and Quarter horses. It has not been easy for "city slickers" like us. Meanwhile, we gradually developed The Elijah Company to the point where it can support us. None of us knew how to do any of this several years ago, and we are still not experts at it. The point of it all is that we wanted to create a learning environment for our children and we have slowly but surely moved towards the context we feel will nurture what we want them to learn.

Since then our priorities have changed. The boys were elementary and middle school ages when we moved to our farm. Now, two have graduated and left home and the third is finishing his time with us. As the boys grew, their interests changed, and now they are not as involved with horses, the outdoors, and construction as they once were. So they gradually moved from a lifestyle of clearing land, driving a tractor, and building a barn and sheds to a lifestyle of designing web sites, performing in musical theater and dance, earning the requirements

---

THERE HAS NEVER BEEN ANOTHER TIME IN HISTORY WHEN CHILDREN SEE SO LITTLE OF THEIR FATHERS.

---

for Eagle Scout, and playing guitar in a worship group. The farm has served its purpose for them, and now the only one actively using the land is me because I'm still breeding Quarter horses. But no matter how things changed, we always tried to create the settings, surroundings, or circumstances that would nurture "true or exact meaning" in our children's lives.

A second, very precious commodity we have tried to give our children is time–time to develop their giftings, time to find God's direction for their lives.

KEY ELEMENTS OF A NURTURING CONTEXT

Here are some elements of a nurturing context:

A lifestyle that reinforces our goals, vision, and purpose for each child
We can only reinforce our goals, vision, and purpose if we protect the unit value of our family. This means a lifestyle centered around home and the family. Is our lifestyle so hectic that our house seems to have revolving doors because everyone is coming and going all the time? Relationships and skills can only be developed within the context of

sustained family time together and a lifestyle that prioritizes family above everything else. Marilyn Howshall in *Wisdom's Way of Learning* says, "It is wise to regard all outside activity simply as an extension of what occurs in the family unit."

A learning environment attuned to the individual

There are many ways we can make our surroundings a "learning environment." We can develop a family library of books, music, art, and so forth. We can allow each child to collect a personal library of his/her favorites. We can design rooms of our home in such a way that they promote learning or have designated "learning centers" throughout the house.

SCHOOLING DOES NOT CONSIDER THE INNATE APTITUDES OR INDIVIDUAL DIFFERENCES THAT ARE CRUCIAL TO CHILDREN'S ABILITIES TO LEARN.

We can have cabinets, bookcases, file cabinets, sets of drawers, and other pieces of furniture that encourage displaying of collections, building personal libraries, keeping mementos, organizing artwork or written work. We can provide tools and raw materials for projects. We can make our yard a place that enhances learning and creative play and provides opportunities for meaningful work. If we are sensitive to our children's interests and the ways in which each child learns best, we can create a learning environment that is best suited for them. The key word in creating a learning environment is "rich."

We want our children's surroundings rich in learning opportunities. As we develop a learning environment, we want to take into account our children's learning styles. Each person has a dominant or preferred way of receiving information. Determining your child's learning preferences can be important because traditional teaching approaches and materials favor the more serious and deliberate temperaments, visual and auditory learners, left-brained thinkers, and students with linguistic and logical- mathematical intelligences. This means that children with different learning preferences find it more difficult to learn in traditional school situations and with traditional teaching materials.

Organizational methods that smooth the way for important activities
All real learning creates clutter and a certain amount of disorganization. We need to find systems of management that work for us and that allow us to nurture learning with the least amount of stress and clutter. We have tried many ways of organizing and have concluded that everyone needs the following:

A way to bring order to the physical surroundings. This is usually some form of chore chart that determines who does which chores when and that also provides a system of accountability through rewards or penalties.

A way to manage time. The best time management tool we have found is a weekly family meeting during which we discuss all the activities for the next week, including lessons, appointments, projects, and our personal "wish lists." We post the family activities and appointments on a write-on/wipe off calendar on the refrigerator and write the personal activities (school lesson plans, individual projects, special work assignments, etc.) in individual notebooks or lesson planners. Other home schoolers do best with a master schedule.

A record-keeping system. This system should allow you to keep track of the children's learning with the least amount of frustration and should cover not only academic areas, but also relational and skill areas.

A schedule. Most states require 36 weeks of classroom instruction (180 days) and a typical school year runs from September to June. Because of health problems and because we travel quite a bit with our business, we have had to adopt a more flexible schedule where we home school year round and take off when we need to. Other home schooling parents have developed different schedules such as on-three weeks, off a week or on-six weeks, off-two weeks or teaching 45 four day weeks with 7 weeks off as needed.

Activities and disciplines that reinforce learning

We live in a culture that has a "Renaissance Man" mind set where everyone is expected to know a little bit about everything, but few people know anything really well. Our educational system is set up to produce "dabblers" who have been exposed to a lot of information but graduate knowing very little of it. Because of this mind set, most home schooling parents tend to do too much academically, because they are worried that their children may have "information gaps." They become so worried about information gaps that they tend to leave relational and life skill gaps. We need to decide which subjects our children will dabble in, which they will participate in, and what they will master. The rule is: Do much of a few things.

In *Wisdom's Way of Learning* Marilyn Howshall encourages us to consider the key activities and disciplines of each subject or skill and to make the child's attitude, efforts, and delight in the work more important than the quantity of work done. We can identify activities and disciplines that reinforce what we want our children to learn relationally, skill-wise, and academically and incorporate those into our lifestyles.

Activities that legitimize and identify

We live in a "sandwich" generation. Many of us were poorly prepared for adulthood and have spent most of our lives building the relationships, mastering the skills, and learning the information necessary for effective living. Yet we are expected to be able to train the next generation. So we are "sandwiched" between a generation that did not pass on to us what we needed in life and a generation that wants us to pass on to them what they need. As the Bible says, we are a generation who must "build up the ancient ruins" and "restore the cities to dwell in." Even though we have never been taught how to do this, we must help our children find the purposes for which they have been created and equip them to accomplish these purposes.

OUR EDUCATIONAL SYSTEM IS SET UP TO PRODUCE "DABBLERS" WHO HAVE BEEN EXPOSED TO A LOT OF INFORMATION BUT GRADUATE KNOWING VERY LITTLE OF IT.

An attitude that balances the process and the product

Traditional schooling focuses on short term results. Its methods are geared to efficiency, not effectiveness. Because the learning process is seen merely as a means to an end, whatever produces results in the shortest amount of time with the greatest number of students is considered a success. Of course, the product is often nothing more than the ability to temporarily recall random bits of information for a test. This kind of learning can be mass produced. What can't be mass produced is the mastering of skills, the ability to apply information, and the development of relationships. Skills, relationships, and application of knowledge cannot be rushed or "crammed," because the process is often more important than the product.

We don't want to be "ever learning but never coming to the knowledge of the truth," but we also don't want to be so product oriented that we force the process. We must find a balance between process and product. If we force the process our children will react either with resistance or resignation. If we prolong the process our children will become bored and restless or discouraged. We want to provide them with a quality process and a quality product.

A recognition of the importance of the father
We are always amazed at the number of families we meet where the extent of Dad's involvement in their home school is "That's nice, honey." In these families the mother is doing the teaching, training, and raising of the next generation of fathers. The "That's nice, honey" Dads are physically, mentally, spiritually, and emotionally absent from the learning process of their children, and home schooling is "Mom's thing." This might work if education is just a process of filling children's heads with information, but it definitely won't work if the family wants to focus on relationships and skills as well as on academics.

Because we are used to the modern American family, we don't realize that the concept of man's sphere being at the office and woman's sphere being at home is relatively new. Even newer is the concept of both parents being away from home during the day, and of the family's livelihood being centered outside of the home. There has never been another time in history when children see so little of their fathers. Prior to the Industrial Revolution the father was the paternal administrator of the family; he led the home and the Church; and he was intimately involved in and directly responsible for the raising of his children (and this included being responsible for their education and preparation for a trade). After the Industrial Revolution, as fathers took jobs outside of the home, for the first time in history children were under the direct supervision of women until they reached adulthood. Nowadays, most children have very little interaction with men and are surrounded by female authority figures at home, at school, and at church.

If Dad is not actively involved in raising and educating his children, the children will think of home schooling as "Mom's thing." Dad is the one who legitimizes the process in the eyes of the children, who places God's blessing upon it, and who imparts vital life skills, particularly to his sons.

A life filled with margin
Our culture encourages us to live beyond our means financially, emotionally, physically, and spiritually. Many of us are under-rested and overwhelmed, feeling constant stress and time pressure. What we need is margin, a term used by author Richard Swenson to describe the space that should exist between where we are and our limits. Margin is having time, energy, and money to spare. It is having physical, emotional, and spiritual reserves. Margin is living within our limits.

In order to fully give ourselves to the important things in our own lives and in the lives of our children we will need the time, energy, and money to create the context that supports our vision of home schooling and the physical, emotional, and spiritual reserves to make the vision a reality.

A focus on the truly important.
We once read a powerful stroy. A speaker stood behind a table on which were a large jar and a container of rocks. He filled the jar with rocks

and asked if the audience thought the jar was full. When they replied, "Yes," he took a box of pebbles from under the table and managed to fit many of them through the spaces between the large rocks. Was the jar full? The audience replied, "Yes." But the speaker produced a canister of sand and filtered a great deal of sand into the jar between the large and small rocks. Finally, he showed that the full jar could hold even more by pouring a pitcher of water into it. The moral of this demonstration is that you must put the big rocks in first. If you start by putting pebbles, sand, or water in the jar, the big rocks won't fit. The "big rocks" of life must be dealt with first or smaller things will crowd them out. Our focus should be on things that are truly important, such as crisis prevention, building relationships, reflective time, renewal of vision, learning new skills, planning, studying, and moving toward goals. There are so many activities, interests, opportunities, and problems vying for our attention that we can easily get sidetracked if we don't stay focused on what is truly important.

CONDITIONS THAT EFFECT LEARNING

An old story tells of the creation of a school for the animals. In this school, everybody took the same four courses: flying, swimming, climbing, and running. Among the students were a duck, a flying squirrel, a fox, and an elephant. These four were highly motivated, and wanted to get good grades, so they all tried very hard.

The duck did fantastically well in swimming and flying, but he lagged behind his classmates in climbing and running, so focused special attention on those two subjects. However, his feet became so sore from trying to run and his wings were so bedraggled from trying to climb that by the end of the year he not only failed both those subjects, but made C's in swimming and flying, which had once been his two best subjects.

At the beginning of the school year, the squirrel was first in his class in climbing and running and was second only to the duck at flying. But as the months wore on, he missed so much school from catching pneumonia in his swimming class that he failed everything. To make matters even worse, because the squirrel constantly squirmed and chattered in class, and had difficulty paying attention, he was diagnosed with a learning disorder. The squirrel eventually was placed in remedial classes and had to be medicated in order to continue with his school work.

The fox was a natural in his running class and scored well in climbing and swimming, but became so frustrated at his inability to get good grades in flying that he began assaulting his classmates. He even tried to eat the duck. His behavior was so disruptive he was expelled from school. He fell in with a rough crowd and eventually wound up in a center for animal delinquents.

The elephant, meanwhile, developed low self-esteem because he couldn't do well in any of the subjects. When he sank into clinical depression, his therapist persuaded him to try a different school that focused on subjects such as lifting and carrying. The elephant was disappointed, because careers in lifting and carrying were not as prestigious as careers in flying, swimming, climbing, or running. Even though he always felt inferior, he managed to make a decent living and support his family.

Our Children are Individuals

The point of this silly story about a school for the animals is that modern education sends every child through a program of study that is targeted toward a "generic" child. It expects every student to be able to follow the same course of study in the same sequence, without considering innate aptitudes or individual differences that are crucial to a child's abilities to learn. Schooling also does not take into account differing personality types or temperaments.

Parents who understand learning differences can be more sympathetic with the frustrations their children face in school and more helpful in finding alternative approaches. The two major learning differences among children have to do with learning styles and learning readiness.

LEARNING STYLES

Each person has a dominant or preferred way of receiving information. People also have different ways in which they process input, different innate aptitudes, and different temperaments. These differences in learning styles can profoundly affect their ability to lean.

A Visual learner is one who learns best through visual images, pictures, diagrams, etc. and by watching others do something. Visual learners tend to be print oriented and can learn by reading about a subject. Some visual learners are strictly Print learners. Auditory learners do better with lectures, songs, stories and other oral material. Kinesthetic learners favor interacting with what they are learning by doing and touching. Most young children are kinesthetic learners, but oftentimes boys will continue to need "hands-on" materials when older. Social or Group Interactive learners learn best through conversations, discussion, and group participation.

A child will give you clues as to which kind of a learner he is not only in his activities but also in the words he uses to express himself. If a child observes and remembers details, likes beautiful things and bright illustrations, and tends to express himself with phrases such as "Look at this!" or "I see what you mean," that child is probably a visual learner. If the child often sings to himself or makes up songs, can remember what people say, and uses expressions like, "Listen to this!" or "I hear what you're saying" to mean he understands, he may be an auditory learner. The child who likes to touch everything, take things apart, and uses expressions like, "I get it" is most likely a kinesthetic learner.

In addition to one or two favored learning styles, each person has a dominant thinking style dependent on whether he or she processes information with the right or the left hemisphere of the brain. Left hemisphere thinking is sequential, analytical, rational, and interested in details. Right hemisphere thinking is "whole concept," intuitive, subjective, and artistic.

Another component of learning is what scientists call The Seven Intelligences. Different people have various innate abilities that make certain studies easier for them. This innate aptitude may be musical, artistic, logical-mathematical, linguistic, bodily-kinesthetic, interpersonal, or intra-personal. Linguistic Intelligence is the ability to use and understand language;

Logical-Mathematical Intelligence is the ability to use numbers and math concepts. Visual-Spacial Intelligence is the ability to understand the relationships of images and figures in space. Musical-Rhythmic Intelligence is the ability to hear tone and pitch and to sense rhythm. Bodily-Kinesthetic Intelligence is the ability to move with grace and strength. Interpersonal Intelligence is the ability to work with other people and lead them. Intra-personal Intelligence is the ability to understand one's own emotions, motivations, and goals. People who have highly developed intelligence in one area may be weak in other areas.

In addition, a child's temperament and his spiritual gifting can have a powerful influence on his ability to learn. Profound differences in people's personalities cause them to be more receptive to certain learning environments and methods.

Determining your child's learning preferences can be important because traditional teaching methods and materials favor the serious and deliberate temperaments, visual and auditory learners, left-brained thinkers, and linguistic and logical-mathematical intelligences.

GOD HAS GIVEN YOU YOUR CHILDREN AND HE WILL GIVE YOU THE WISDOM, PATIENCE, AND LOVE TO DO WHAT IS BEST FOR THEM.

LEARNING READINESS

Dr. Raymond Moore was part of a task force of leading American educators who studied early childhood learning for the U. S. Office of Economic Opportunity. Based on his years of research, Dr. Moore reached two conclusions about learning readiness:

[1] Many children suffer needless physical, emotional, and mental stress because they are placed in academic settings before their vision, hearing, nervous system, reasoning abilities, and muscular coordination are developed enough to complete conventional schooling tasks.

[2] Children are often taught academic skills before they have enough life experiences and background knowledge to grasp the concepts involved.

Dr. Moore and his wife, Dorothy, have since become two of America's leading advocates of home education. They have written many books encouraging parents to delay formal education until children are mentally, physically and emotionally ready.

A COMFORTABLE LEARNING ENVIRONMENT

In addition to learning styles and readiness, a "student-friendly" environment is critical to learning. "Student-friendly" environments take into consideration the child's physical and emotional surroundings. Children learn best in a positive, affirming atmosphere with enjoyable surroundings where they are physically and emotionally secure.

Many children are sensitive to lighting, to room temperature, to visual distractions such as clutter, to auditory distractions such as background noise, and to whether the seating is comfortable. Some students work better alone, while others do their best work when other people are involved Children are also sensitive to their teacher's attitudes toward them. Children who are expected to fail often do poorly in school, while children who are expected to succeed generally are better learners. Observant parents can create a physical and emotional environment in which each child does his or her best work.

TEACHING STYLES

The way information is presented also has a powerful effect on learning. Teachers tend to have a favorite "teaching style" such as lecturing, assigning workbook pages, providing "hands-on" activities, etc. Sometimes the teacher's teaching style or the way the information is presented clashes with the way the student learns best. Many learning specialists are discovering that children are often labeled "learning disabled" when actually the teaching method frustrates their ability to learn.

SOME THOUGHTS ABOUT GENDER IDENTITY

We live in the age of unisex haircuts, unisex clothes, and unisex lifestyles. It is an age when the lines of distinction between male and female have been blurred. We believe God created male and female as distinct sexes with different aptitudes, attitudes, destinies, and life-styles. We also believe that it is in our best interest to live within God's plan for who we are. If we don't, our lives are constantly out of sync with the deepest level of reality and this continual dissonance results in turmoil.

How can we restore Christian manhood and womanhood? First, by recognizing what we've lost. Modern culture has stripped men, and consequently boys, of many masculinizing influences. Most boys are surrounded by female authority figures at home, at school, and at church, and the tasks demanded of them (being still and quiet, being verbal and visual, using fine motor skills, concentrating for a long period of time) are tasks at which girls excel. Generations of boys have been humiliated because they physically and academically were expected to act like girls. In addition, there has never been another time in history when children see so little of their fathers. No wonder boys don't know how to become men. Daddy is never around to teach them. Both Christians and non-Christians are recognizing feminizing influences on modern men and are asking "What makes a man?"

On the other side of the coin, modern women are faced with options their ancestors never could have imagined. Just as there has been a feminizing of boys, there has been a masculinizing of girls. As men have abdicated their roles of leader, provider, and protector, women have filled the gaps. In addition, our country is still suffering the effects of the Civil War, which decimated the male population and left a lasting legacy of female leadership in the home, school, and church.

The second thing we need to do is create a context where our sons and daughters become true Christian men and women. Fathers need to be actively involved in every facet of their children's lives, particularly in the lives of their sons. Sons need opportunities to be involved in masculine activities that require hard physical labor, mechanical skill, leadership, and intellectual excellence. Sports and recreation are poor substitutes for traditional masculine activities.

Daughters need the love and affirmation of their fathers, but also need mothers who model biblical womanhood. We need to be careful not to plant seeds in our daughters that will later make them dissatisfied with the roles of wife and mother. This doesn't mean women can't be enterprising. The Proverbs 31 woman had a lot of irons in the fire that would put many modern professional men to shame. It also doesn't mean being a wife and mother are the only options. Many great servants of God were single women. The issue is a feminine spirit whether or not the attitudes and actions model a true representation of biblical womanhood.

BRINGING YOUR CHILD HOME

Home schooling is always interesting, but for those bringing children home from public school it can be a real challenge. Some of the most common problems are:

Peer Dependency. Children who have spent eight hours each day with friends usually have begun looking to their peers for advice, direction, an assessment of their self-worth, and an idea of how to behave. Peer dependent children may react to being home schooled in a variety of ways ranging from resisting instruction to feeling their lives have been ruined. Even children who happily anticipated home schooling will experience difficulty transferring their loyalties from friends to family.

Parents also suffer from peer dependency and feel pressured by friends or family to use certain teaching materials and methods or to produce a certain level of academic achievement.

Distorted Self-Esteem. The classroom can distort a child's self-esteem in two ways. If the child is unattractive, uncoordinated, has peculiar habits, or is slow to catch on to academics, he or she has probably been ridiculed and ostracized by classmates and teachers. He/she may carry labels ranging from "dumb" to "weird" to "Attention Deficit Disorder." On the other hand, the popular child who has made good grades has learned to derive personal worth from looks, athletics, or academic performance. Parents will have to deal with their own lack of confidence and inexperience and may never have recovered from their own childhood "labels."

Burn Out. Public school gives many children (and gave their par-

---

LOOK FOR SOLUTIONS IN YOUR HEART BEFORE YOU LOOK FOR THEM IN YOUR HEAD.

---

ents) a "dullness" or apathy towards learning. The child's natural love of learning may have been badly damaged from too much busywork and the forced learning of too many things that serve no real purpose in life. Damage also stems from inappropriate schoolwork that demanded skills the child had not yet developed. Boys are more likely to be frustrated by schoolwork because their fine motor skills, verbal abilities, and thinking processes are slow to develop. For boys then, the classroom may have been a place of great frustration, humiliation, and failure. Many boys who come home to school dislike anything having to do with books.

Mom will also have to beware of "burn out." Mothers who are not used to having their children around 24 hours a day and who are unprepared for the changes in lifestyle that home schooling brings may find themselves emotionally and physically strung out.

SOME SOLUTIONS

If you are experiencing problems in your home school, look for solutions within your heart before you look for them in your head. You are dealing with "heart" problems, not "head" problems; problems that involve wounded spirits and damaged emotions. So before you attach your own labels to your children ("disrespectful," "rebellious," "lazy," etc.), take time to assess the situation from the Lord's point of view and also from the child's point of view.

Resistance is not necessarily rebellion

Not only have your child's classmates encouraged him to disrespect your authority, but the very nature of the institutional school insinuates that parents know nothing and are not reliable sources of information. So you will have to spend some time rebuilding trust and receptivity to you in your child.

Another source of resistance is frustration. What you think is rebellion may actually be your child's frustration with material that is too difficult for him. Your way of teaching may clash with his learning style or have unpleasant associations from the past. The child may be "burned out" and not emotionally capable of tackling more schoolwork yet. There also may be patterns of behavior that brought him attention in the classroom. When you try and change this behavior at home, the child may react negatively.

Many parents who have taken a child out of public school, especially if the child was labeled with a learning disorder, have found that they must spend the first year healing the child's wounded spirit and establishing a context of loving acceptance and encouragement. Only then can real learning occur.

Get help from Dad

The less involved Dad is with the home school, the more resistant children tend to become (especially the boys). If a boy associates learning with femininity (women teachers, women in charge, women making the decisions), he basically has two choices: become effeminately compliant or assert his masculinity improperly. Fathers can help their sons learn productive and respectful ways to assert their masculinity. A Dad's active involvement in the home school also communicates to his children that Dad considers this a very important endeavor.

Look at the challenges as opportunities

God has given you your children and He will give you the wisdom, patience, and love to do what is best for them. Sometimes there are no answers to the "Why God?" questions of our lives, but even the worst situations are opportunities to trust God and to believe that He is in control no matter what the evidence may be to the contrary.

13

HOMESCHOOLING IS NOT ABOUT EDUCATION

IN CHAPTER 2, WE OUTLINED the reasons families choose to homeschool, and in Chapter 5 we discussed the three types of homeschoolers: pioneers, settlers and refugees. I would now like to take this opportunity to bring us back to what I perceive to be the reason God began this movement over 20 years ago.

As I have described the three kinds of homeschoolers in Chapter 5, you may have noticed a very subtle, yet most important, difference between the Pioneers' main desire (to have their children grow up at home) and the main desire of the other two groups (to provide a better education or a less negative context for their children).

The reason I entitled this article, "Homeschooling is Not About Education" is because I think we have a tendency to lose sight of or, perhaps we have never really understood, why we were led to homeschool. I draw this conclusion because what I hear as most homeschooling parents' primary concerns are issues such as, "Will this be the best curriculum for my child?" or, "How do I know I'm going to cover it all?"

Let's take another look at this thing called "homeschooling." We all know one or more families whose children would greatly benefit if their children were not in a public school setting. Yet, these families don't bring their children home. We feel truly blessed to believe in homeschooling and we don't understand why everyone doesn't see the obvious benefits. Why do friends and relatives keep sending their children to "school," anyway? Why do we seem to be among so few who are willing to do this?

I would like to offer my opinion as to why we have become "homeschoolers" and so many others have not: I have a conviction that an historical time is approaching for which a certain "kind" of person will be needed in this nation; indeed, in the world. When this time will come, I don't know, but my sense is that it will come soon. What I do believe is that God has needed a very specific context within which He can grow up this particular kind of person. This context is a family that is very different from the kind of families existing in our society today. It is a place where the hearts of the fathers have been turned toward their children and the hearts of the children have been turned toward their fathers. It is a place where children are raised to become proficient at the specific giftings, talents, and callings God has placed within them since their creation.

This is the context of the homeschooling family. Yet, what disturbs me is that home-SCHOOLING has become of such importance, homeschooling parents are prioritizing something quite different than what was in the hearts of those early Pioneers when they brought (or kept) their children home during the day.

For those of you who have "brought the school home," let me suggest that you rethink what you are really doing with your children. Do you ever consider what kind of person this little boy or girl is to become by the time he or she leaves your home? Have you ever wondered if God, Himself, has placed some very specific talents, giftings and callings in this youngster that He expects you to discover and promote during the child's stay with you? Do such things determine your family's priorities, weekly schedule or the curricula you purchase?

Or, as you look toward the "finish line" of your child's time at home, do you simply buy a graded curricula and spend your days plowing through it, because you think the highest purpose of your parenting is to see that your child receive the best education you can provide so you can one day say, "My son has a good job."

LET ME SUGGEST THAT YOU RETHINK WHAT YOU ARE REALLY DOING WITH YOUR CHILDREN.

If the answers to these questions are something like, "I don't know"; or, "I don't want to think about it," then you may be a "homeschooler;" but I think you've missed the point.

Even Pioneers can slowly become Refugees. The very word "homeschooling" can cause us all to forget that what we are doing is not about home-SCHOOLING but about creating that context in which we assist God in raising the little ones in our homes to become His men and women who are truly prepared for what comes next.

My definition of "Pioneer" as described in Chapter 5 is: Parents who have taken total responsibility for raising (including educating) their own children, personally, academically and spiritually; normally meaning having them at home during the "school day." Pioneers do not give over any of this responsibility to another. Pioneers may reach into the community, including the school system and church for assistance in this effort; but, parents always assume full responsibility for the ultimate outcome.

Is it realistic for parents to be Pioneers during their children's High School years?

Actually, it is during the child's High School years that parents discover if they really do have the heart of a Pioneer. Consider that the very concept of "High School" (as well as the concept of "adolescence") is not a biblical idea. It was created for the benefit of helping the institutional educational model be more efficient. It does not have to drive the way we raise our children.

Both the concepts of High School and "Teenagers" are an invention of our modern era. What did parents do with their children—how did they truly understand them—before there was High School and before there were Teenagers? (This last sentence said tongue-in-cheek)

It is "context" and not "education" that is the reason God had families bring (or keep) their children home. Of course we educate, but not out of fear, nor is education our priority. Here is the key: "What are the real priorities in our homes?" In other words, "Yes we are preparing our children; but, for what?"

Children lose when parents don't have a clear vision for what they are really trying to accomplish. It's simply easier to "bring home the school" along with the child than to ask God what this is all about. I confess that it's taken 20 years for me to come to enough understanding of why we are homeschooling so that I could put it into words myself.

Even Pioneers can slowly become Settlers (or, even Refugees), especially when their children became "High School" age. There are Refugees who come to the revelation of what God is doing and instantly became Pioneers. Then there are those who have homeschooled a long time before understanding what God is doing. Our family falls into this latter category.

For several weeks when my youngest son was 16, I could not decide what was going on with him and concluded that I had no choice but to put him in public school. He didn't want to go, but I was pulling out what little hair I still had. Then, one day, I asked myself, "Wait a minute. What do I *really* believe here?" I slowed down enough to give it some thought. I listened to Mary Hood's seminar tapes. I had a long conversation with my son in which I shared how much I appreciated the kind of person he had become, what I saw as the budding gifts and talents God had placed within him, and how good he was becoming in those areas. Who changed? I did. We immediately got back on track.

14

IDENTITY DIRECTED HOMESCHOOLING

MOST OF US WHO homeschool strive to give our children positive experiences with relationships and try to limit their exposure to people and circumstances that reinforce teen rebellion. So why, in home-schooling families, do we have children who begin to pull away from their parents as they reach puberty? I have watched this happen time after time in close-knit Christian families, and I have also seen the stress this causes between parents and children. Even when the child-parent relationship seems strong, children can begin to develop a sense of "otherly-ness" when they reach the teen years, and too often parents interpret this "pulling away" as rebellion or rejection. Is this a sign of rebellion or rejection of the family values we parents have so carefully guarded? I want to suggest another interpretation of this often painful time in the lives of teens and their parents.

I don't consider my children's teen years a time to simply endure, as in "This too shall pass." Instead, I prefer to say that these are the "Years of Identification." I use this phrase because I believe that too many parents dislike and fear adolescence; but if they understood the dynamics of the teen years, they would look forward to them with real excitement.

I believe that when God gives a child to parents, that child comes prepackaged with a set of giftings and callings uniquely his or her own. Inside that child is a seed which, if properly nourished, will grow up into the mature expression of what is within that seed. Just as simply as an acorn (which looks nothing at all like an oak tree) becomes an oak tree under the right conditions, so a child will (under the right conditions) grow up to become exactly the person his Father created him to become.

Christians don't speak much of "destiny" anymore, mainly because it has become a catch-word among humanists and New Agers. But we need to look again at the concept of destiny. The Bible is full of hints that each one of us is created for a specific time and purpose in God's unfolding plan. Ephesians 2: 10 even says we each have "good works which God predestined for us" before the world was ever created. Before time began, God had your son or daughter on His mind, He chose your child, and He prearranged a life for him or her to live. So parents, those teenagers in your home are not just biological events. They are beings pre-determined by God and destined to, just as the Bible says of David, "serve their generation well."

During the teen years, children begin to realize they are not just extensions of their parents, but have their own identities and destinies. When the child's developing identity is very different from the parents' expectations, there can be a lot of relational grief and adversity. Family tensions are compounded because the child (being a child) will tend to express his still developing identity in immature and inappropriate ways. If you want a biblical example of an adolescent who created family tensions because he had a special destiny, just read the story of Joseph. He must have been one obnoxious teen!

I have seen much that is adversarial in home-schooling a teen be nothing more than the parents' inability to let go of personal expectations and accept what God may be creating in the child, even though that creation is still very rough around the edges. We may have dreams of our children following certain careers (like becoming missionary

> **PERHAPS THE BIGGEST FEAR OF HOMESCHOOLING PARENTS IS THAT THEIR CHILDREN WILL HAVE LEARNING "GAPS", THAT SOMETHING WILL BE LEFT OUT OF THEIR CHILD'S EDUCATION.**

doctors), or having certain temperaments (compliant, sensitive to the needs of others, respectful), or excelling at certain skills (like math or science or music), or even accomplishing one of our goals (like getting a basketball scholarship to college). When a child doesn't follow our dreams, and even seems resistant to fulfill them, it is easy to form negative opinions: he's lazy, he's not trying, he's resistant, he doesn't have any initiative, he's rebellious, he's uncooperative, and so on. The simple truth may be that we are forcing the child to fit a mold he was never created to fill, and his spirit is reacting to the pressure. We are trying to make our child into something he was never meant to be. There are a thousand little ways we may be doing this from forcing him to have the same interests we have, to trying to make him become involved in activities we wish we could have been involved in when we were young, to sending him through a course of study that has nothing to do with what God Himself wants this child to prioritize educationally. Could we actually be violating our child's spirit by pressuring him to become someone God never meant him to be? Could the resistance we see simply be his way of coping with the pressure? When a child becomes resistant, resentful, or obnoxious, and we parents are tempted to label them as rebellious and disrespectful, we should ask ourselves, "What's really going on here? Is there something God has placed in this child that we are not respecting and encouraging? Is he struggling with a sense of destiny that leads him in a different direction than the direction we are trying to make him go? Is his way of being a person different from our way?"

THREE IMPORTANT KINDS OF TRUST

First, we must trust God that He knows what He is doing. He has put this "seed" of identity and destiny in our child. Can we trust that He is capable of bringing that seed to fruition, and trust that He will "clue us in" about who our child really is and whether what we are dealing with is identity-related or is truly rebellion?

Second, we must trust ourselves that all of our effort to be good parents and give our children a nurturing, Christian upbringing will ultimately be rewarded, even though we made plenty of mistakes.

Third, we must trust our child, and this is the hardest kind of trust to have. It is also very humbling, because this kind of trust requires us to relax our parent roles where we are "large and in charge" and become more like older brothers or sisters in Christ to our sons and daughters. We must trust that all the good and godly input we gave over the years actually lodged in our child's heart, and is really in there, even though we can't see any evidence of it. We must also trust that God will produce a deep enough relationship between Him and our child so that the child can actually grow up knowing how to hear from God and respond to Him, even though that response may be expressed in foolish or immature ways. When we start trusting our children's relationships with the Lord, we allow them to have more and more say in who they are and what they want to do with their time, and we begin respecting their individuality.

We have all heard the biblical injunction to "Train up a child in the way he should go and when he is old he will not depart from it." Most often this Bible verse in Proverbs is used to justify moral training, but that is not all the verse is about.

The Hebrew word which is translated "to train up" is also used in another place in the Bible. When Solomon dedicated the Temple, the word translated "dedicate" is the same Hebrew word used in the Proverbs verse as "train up." This Hebrew word means to "discriminate," to "narrow the focus." Simply put, as a child grows up, we parents should be continually narrowing the focus of this child's set of educational and practical experiences to be more and more specific to who this child was created to be. When "dedicated" (the focus narrowed, or the Temple identified as to what it really was), the Temple could never again be considered whatever those watching might have speculated was being constructed in their midst. It was the Temple of God! It was not a racquetball court, a school, or the king's palace.

God created your child. He gave this future young man or young woman a potential relationship with Him as well as something to do for his or her generation. Then He gave the child to you. As the years go by, He will let you know who this child is to become. Each child is different. Some children are so different from the other members of their families that parents can hardly comprehend how to best help them. Parents should pay attention to each of their children and ask the Creator to constantly give them insight into who each child is. Slowly, but surely, the Spirit of God (that unseen Presence) in your home will let you know His design for each child you are raising. With

this growing knowledge, you will be able to give that child an individualized set of growing-up experiences tailored to his specific needs,
and one which will prepare him to fully become the person God had
in mind before the foundation of the world.

When you are "narrowing the focus" so that you concentrate
on certain things, you will have to leave other things "out of focus;" you will have to let go of the "good" for the sake of the "best."

> **"I SAW THE ANGEL IN THE MARBLE**
> **AND I CARVED UNTIL I SET HIM FREE."**
> **—MICHELANGELO**

Perhaps the biggest fear of homeschooling parents is that their children will have learning "gaps" that something will be left out of their
child's education. Because of this, and because our society promotes
over-achievement, parents tend to try and cover too much, to make
their children knowledgeable about everything. The better approach
would be to use the elementary years to build a general academic foundation, but then continually "narrow the focus" as the children grow
older and as the parents have a better understanding of each child's
unique skills, interests, and giftings.

It takes both time and resources to be good at anything. Helping a
child find his identity means money must be spent on resources and experiences. It means time must be spent paying attention to the child's
personality, abilities, and likes and dislikes. It means emotional energy
must be spent working through the inevitable relational problems that
arise from trying to get to know children as people, not just as "kids."

It also means giving your children the large blocks of time they need to become good at whatever it is they need to master.

There is a story about the artist, Michelangelo. It is said that he would order a large block of marble and have it placed where he would have plenty of room to walk around it. Michelangelo would spend days staring at the marble. People would watch Michelangelo and think he was very strange. Picture this man, hour by hour, day by day, looking at a large piece of marble. What was he doing? One thing he was not doing was considering what he would carve out of the marble.

Finally, Michelangelo went to work. One of his creations was what is known today as Michelangelo's Angel, a beautifully intricate angel with remarkable detail.

What was Michelangelo doing all those days he walked around the block of marble, looking intently at the stone? What he was doing was waiting until the marble told him what was inside.

How do I know this? It's because, when Michelangelo was finished carving the angel he said, "I saw the angel in the marble and I carved until I set him free."

May I suggest that this is exactly what we do with our children: We are constantly and intently observing each of our children until we "see" what God created and put inside them. As we are able to identify what God has created—as we see the specific talents, giftings and callings God wants the child to manifest as he or she grows up—we then give that child the time and the resources to become really good at those talents, giftings and callings. We may not see an "angel" in the child; but, we will see what God has put in there because God is more interested in these things being identified than we could possible be.

The final step is that, when we see what is "in there," we turn to the child and tell him or her what we see. I can tell you from my experience with my own children, this is the most important thing we can do for them: Give them an identity.

I hand you an acorn and ask, "Given the right circumstances for its growth, what will this acorn become? If you didn't already know, you would never guess, "An oak tree."

God has given you several different kinds of "seed" in the form of your individual children. What's more, He will tell you what you can expect each "seed" to become. If you will pay attention. And, if you will pay attention, you can make sure each seed grows up to be a full grown, mature, and healthy "tree" that is exactly "after its own seed."

Consider the following statistics:

- The average college student now takes six years to finish a four year degree due to multiple changes in majors; and, and 40% never finish at all.
- Only 10-15% of those who finish college go on to work in the field for which they spent years and thousands of dollars preparing.
- The average American changes jobs seven times and has three complete career changes.
- Many adults, especially men, experience a period of emotional turmoil in mid-life when they question their meaning and purpose. This event is so common that society has coined a term for it: "mid-life crisis."

How do I interpret these statistics? One thing seems fairly obvious to me. Ours is a generation of individuals who don't know who they are or why they are on this planet! I don't want my sons to contribute to these statistics. I would like to believe each boy could enter adult-hood with a fairly clear sense of identity and having had the time, resources, and emotional support to become really good at what God has placed within him to do.

Our three sons have never known what it means to be "institutionally educated". Our eldest graduated in 1999 and the second oldest graduated in 2000. All my sons are walking with the Lord. As the boys entered puberty, they no longer saw themselves as mere extensions of Mom and Dad. They began to develop a personality, character, and dominant traits that said, "I am someone different and not just an extension of you." The way they expressed their differences was often

---

LET US SEEK TO IDENTIFY OUR CHILDREN AND GIVE THEM THE GREAT EDGE OTHERS LEAVE HOME WITHOUT.

---

inappropriate and immature and sometimes offensive. So I had to look beyond their behavior and try to distinguish their true identities. I could look beyond their behavior because I believe two things: First I believe that my sons are going to be men of God, which means they are not just my sons but also are my brothers in Christ. Second, I believe my sons, imperfect as they may be, genuinely want to become men of God. Believing these two things, I can place myself "alongside" them in the role of an encouraging brother as well as "above" them in the role of father who is helping them find out who they are. I can also trust that "He who began a good work" in my sons "will be faithful to complete it."

A special plea to fathers: I am convinced that one of the most important responsibilities a father has is to identify his children. What do I mean by "identify?" I mean that he helps his children know who they really are. Over the years I have realized just how powerful a father's words can be in the lives of his children. We fathers are constantly identifying our children with our words. Unfortunately, many of us speak words which say, in effect, "You are no good. You are not worth much. You will never amount to much. You'll never make it." Over time our children internalize our words of identification and begin thinking: "I am not very smart/good/pretty/worthy, etc."; or, "I am limited" With our words we fathers have not only given our children negative identities, but we have undermined God's identities for them. We had better be speaking to them words God, Himself, would say!

What else do I mean when I talk about a father identifying his children? I mean the father pays attention to what the Holy Spirit reveals as identifying characteristics the child is showing on a daily basis. What does the child like to do in his or her spare time? What toys does the child like, or what is the child good at? What broad areas (such as people skills or mechanical skills) is the child beginning to exhibit? As you see these (often only with an internal eye), take the time to speak words of positive identification to the child, such as "I notice you are really good at working with machinery. You seem to be able to sense what is wrong with a piece of equipment and you can usually figure out how to fix it."

I do this when the boys are together with me (and I make sure this happens often). I will tell Seth, "I am always amazed and impressed when you are able to look at a problem and go right to the source of what's wrong. You may be wondering why I am always calling on you when I can't figure out what's wrong with the computer or lawn mower, etc. That's because I know you can tell me right away. You have tremendous problem-solving skills. I believe you could take just about any problem and solve it."

My second son James may be listening to these words. He knows he cannot do the things Seth can do, and he will begin to feel a little jealous of Seth and how I am able to say such good words to his brother. Everyone needs a benediction. Not flattery, mind you, but exactly what the word "benediction" means (bene: good, diction: word): "good words."

So James may ask, "And what about me, Dad?" I turn to James and say, "James, you are not very good at these things." James knows this already, but he is a little surprised that I would say so. He wants me to say something good about him, too. But part of defining James is to let him know who he is not. He is not a problem-solver, but he has other strengths.

Now I am able to say to James, "The reason you are not very good at the things Seth can do is that God has put in you completely different abilities. James, you are one of the most 'people' persons I know. Even little children follow you around." "Everyone loves you, James, and you are a strong man of God. People watch you, and you give them the courage to trust the Lord in their lives because you, as a young man with many health problems, are trusting in the Lord for your future: a future filled with all things creative, because that's who James is."

When I am through talking to James, he has no desire to be like Seth. He is James, that unique person who is like no one else. And so it is with Blake, and so it should be with each of our children. It is the great responsibility and joy of fathers to do this for their children. It is one way of imparting the "blessing" so often mentioned in the Bible.

Let us seek to identify our children and give them the great edge others leave home without: a sense of who they are meant to become, and the skills to begin on the path of what they came into the world to do.

15

WHATEVER HAPPENED TO CURIOSITY?

"IT WAS MY SON'S first day of school. As he boarded the bus that day, I was as excited as he was. He was such a clever, creative, inquisitive child. I just knew he would thrive in school. Then, one day, several months later, I picked him up at the bus stop. As he slowly stepped off the bus, I suddenly noticed something missing in his eyes. There was no enthusiasm, no spark. It scared me. I said in my heart, 'Who did this to my little boy? Who extinguished his fire!'"

This sad story (or one similar to it) has been experienced countless times since the advent of the public school movement. Maybe you have had a similar experience and that is why your little one doesn't go to school anymore. However, did you know that we can keep our children home and do the same thing to them that has been done to millions of children for over 150 years.

Children come into a world that is filled with wonderful, intriguing; and, yes, sometimes dangerous things. There is an awful lot they need to know. And, there is a whole subculture of trained professionals out there just waiting to get these kids into a room and tell them what they *should* want to know.

The trouble is, children are curious. God built this into them.

They want to know all sorts of stuff. Most of it isn't very important, really. Except to them. What do your children ask you? Their questions are wonderfully creative and, yes, sometimes annoying.

Whether our children are in school or we are "schooling" them at home, most of us believe that what children should learn has already been established. It is simply up to us to make sure all the stuff they are supposed to know actually gets inside of them. But, are these the things our children want to know? If we were honest, we would have to admit the answer would probably be, "No." Of course, we don't ask our children what they are curious about, or what intrigues them, or what they would like to know. After all, who are they? Just kids.

When my sons were younger and our catalog was smaller, I would take an hour or two and read our catalog out loud to them. That's right, I would read our whole catalog, page by page, to the boys. In front of me was a piece of paper divided into three parts. As I read the catalog I encouraged the boys to stop me when something sounded interesting that they thought they might want to learn during the coming year. Then I would type out a list of what each boy indicated he was interested in learning. Of course, each child had way more on his list than could possibly be covered in a school year, so I spent time with each one and we whittled the list down to a manageable size.

"James," I said during one of these sessions. "You have said you want to raise snakes this year." As I had read through the science section of our catalog, I had come to the category on snakes and James had made me put "snakes" on his list. I didn't mind James raising snakes if that is what he truly wanted to do. I just needed him to know, from my own experience as a boy his age, what raising snakes entailed. After listening carefully to me, James said, "OK, Dad, maybe I'll do snakes next year." As the years went by, James never raised snakes, but he also never lost his interest in them. I allowed him to spend as much time as he wanted studying them.

Of course, in order to do this with my children, I had to object to the worldview that what children should learn has already been established. Why? Because if we allow our children to do many of the things that interest them, a lot of time is used up that ordinarily would be spent teaching them the "officially" recognized curriculum.

**THE TROUBLE IS, CHILDREN ARE
CURIOUS. GOD BUILT THIS INTO THEM.
THEY WANT TO KNOW ALL SORTS
OF STUFF. MOST OF IT ISN'T VERY
IMPORTANT, REALLY. EXCEPT TO THEM.**

In their very important book, *Discover Your Child's Learning Style*, authors Willis and Hodson make the following observations:

> *"When children enter the schoolroom in kindergarten or first grade, their abilities to conform and perform according to preset standards are what they are judged by. And, ...conformity and performance measures are what count. Memorizing facts, taking tests, and receiving grades replace investigating, wondering, discovering, playing, and asking questions." (pgs 25-26)*

We assume children will learn what we want them to learn the way we want them to learn it. What is so very dangerous about this assumption is that, for many children, what we *really* want for our

117

children is destroyed in the process: that each child develop a life-long love of learning.

I have written many articles, and spent many years speaking about the one-size-fits-all, graded, generic, in-the-box, prepackaged, scope & sequence curricula that is in use by so many homeschooling families today. This type of curricula was originally produced when the public schooling movement began in the mid 1800's because these are the materials most useful to efficiently educate masses of children in a "factory" model of institutionalized government (or, for that matter, private or Christian) schooling.

In the beginning of the homeschooling movement, "prepackaged" curricula was not available to homeschooling parents. The reason is that in the early years homeschooling parents weren't at all interested in reproducing the activities of public school children. Since home-schooled children weren't using the same materials as children who were "in school", publishers initially didn't see homeschoolers as a "market." But, as the homeschooling movement drew families whose primary concern was their children's education, publishers of public, private, and Christian school curricula found a new market for their traditional, scope & sequence-style curricula. Homeschooling parents began to try to produce the same kind of high school graduate as the public school, so they began using the same curricula. In an institutional school setting, a child's abilities to conform and perform to preset standards are what he or she is judged by. I would like to suggest that, in the homeschool setting, what needs to be judged is the level of curiosity found in our children.

I recently read a study which concluded that 85% of all communication aimed at three year olds is either telling the child not to do something he is doing or how bad he is for having done what he just did. I was astonished. What are all these three year olds doing that they need such continual correction? I would suspect that, most of the time, they are simply being curious. They are exploring, and, in so doing, getting into things they "shouldn't" be getting into. Although I am not a strict believer in the Unschooling approach to home education, one of my favorite quotes comes from John Holt, who was an educator, author and founder of the unschooling movement. Here is what Holt writes in one of his books:

> *What is lovely about children is that they can make such a production, such a big deal, out of anything or nothing. From my office window I see many families walking down the street with their children. The adults plod along. The children twirl, leap, skip, run now to this side, now to that. They look for things to step over or jump over or walk along or around. They climb on anything that can be climbed. I never want to be where I cannot see it.*
>
> *All that energy and foolishness, all that curiosity, questions, talk, all the fierce passions and inconsolable sorrows, immoderate joys, seem to many to be a nuisance to be endured if not a disease to be cured. To me, they are a national asset, a treasure beyond price, more necessary to our health and our very survival than any oil or uranium or name what you will.*
>
> *One day in a public garden I see on a small patch of grass under some trees a father and a two year old girl. The father is lying down. The little girl runs everywhere. What joy to run! Suddenly she stops, looks intently at the ground, bends down, picks something up. A twig!. A pebble! She stands up, runs again. She sees a pigeon and*

chases it. Suddenly she stops and looks up into the sunlit trees. What does she see? Perhaps a squirrel, perhaps a bird, perhaps the shapes and colors of the leaves in the sun. Then she bends down, finds something else, picks it up, examines it. Another miracle!

"Gears! Leaves! Twigs! Little children love the world. That is why they are so good at learning about it. For it is love, not tricks and techniques of thought, that lies at the heart of all true learning. Can we bring ourselves to let children learn through that love?"

ENCOURAGING AND NOURISHING CURIOSITY

Take a piece of paper and draw a line from the left of the page to the right. At the extreme left side of the line, write "birth." At the extreme right of the line, write "leaving home." Somewhere along the line, put "age 12." Now, from birth to about age 12 your child's learning experiences should be as experiential as possible. This is the time for taking ordinary activities (ie. setting the table, building a birdhouse, looking through a microscope) and learning while doing. It is the time to buy lots of field guides and a good microscope. Put a terrarium on the kitchen table (or a counter top) and tell your kids, "Whatever you find outside and don't know what it is, bring it in and put it in the terrarium. We'll get the field guide and look it up." This is the time to raise pets, get to know the stars, and ask thousands of questions.

Thousands of questions? Yes. You should be asking questions constantly. And, you don't even have to know the answers. Just ask. "Why do you suppose grass is green and the sky is blue?" "Why are blue flowers so rare in nature?" "Why do so many animals hide from us?" "What is electricity?" Why should you do this? Because children need to know that asking questions is not only an all right thing to do, it is the best way to be a life-long learner.

If your children hear you asking questions all the time, guess what they will grow up doing? That's right. And, if they grow up asking questions, they may not accept just anything and everything they are told. They might actually be immune to propaganda and advertising. They will think! Today's children don't ask questions because, early in their lives, they are told that grown-ups will eventually tell them everything they need to know.

OUR FIRST PRIORITY IS TO NURTURE THE CHILD'S SENSE OF WONDER.

Men have believed many things for long periods of time that turned out to be untrue when someone decided to question their validity. But, first, someone had to ask. One of Einstein's most famous quotes goes like this, "If the facts don't fit the theory, change the facts." Einstein spent his life questioning accepted scientific beliefs. He also said, "Curiosity is more important than knowledge."

And, we should be asking our children questions about Scripture. If Scripture is the most true of truths, our children's faith will be strengthened the more questions we bring to the Bible. I challenge parents, and I challenge myself, to engender a sense of curiosity in our children. One of the most important words you will ever hear your child say is, "Why?" The second most important word is, "WOW!" This word is full of expression, wonder and inquisitiveness. Eventually, you will need to add academics to your child's experiential learning. Don't begin this too soon and never allow academics to overwhelm curiosity. One can almost see Einstein shaking his head as he wrote,

"It is a miracle that curiosity survives formal education."

The teachers we remember from our own schooling experiences were the ones who challenged us and piqued our curiosity. We might even remember an "out of the box" college professor who made a course or two memorable. Here is something my wife, Ellyn, wrote about a professor she once had:

"When I was in college, my major professor was an herpetologist, more specifically, he was a snake fanatic. On every field trip he expected us to gather as many snakes as possible. In the course of one quarter we went to the Okefenokee Swamp where we collected water snakes, to grasslands where we looked for black racers, to dilapidated farm buildings to find corn snakes and rat snakes, and to various other places where snakes are abundant. But the trip I will never forget was to an island off the Gulf Coast of Florida. Dr. Wharton's specialty was cottonmouth water moccasins, and this island boasts one of the South's densest populations of these creepy creatures. Why? Because ibises (stork-like birds) nest in the scraggly sea grape bushes covering its swamplike interior. Beneath each bush lurks a family of hungry water moccasins, ready to gobble any eggs or chicks that fall from the nests above. We were given burlap sacks, snake sticks (a pole with a noose at one end) and expected to make our contribution to the advancement of herpetology. It was during that field trip—while slogging through the muck, breathing in the acrid odor of ibis dung, jumping at every movement in the bushes, and praying the water moccasins had decided to take the day off—that I changed my major to biochemistry.

"Years later I found myself with three sons, and guess what? Snakes again! It seemed like every time I turned around Seth, James, or Blake would be reaching into a pocket, pulling out something long and wiggly and asking, 'What's this, Mom?' (Having majored in biology, I was supposed to be the expert.) We would pull the field guides down from the shelf and find out the name of each prized catch. I even went to the store and bought an aquarium with a screen top and we made a landscape and populated it with snakes, lizards, frogs, toads, and turtles. Over the years our home has been host to many different reptiles and amphibians and we have studied these interesting creatures at varying levels of intensity.

"Our first priority when we study nature is to nurture the child's sense of wonder. Modern schooling techniques tend to inundate children with predigested information, planned activities, and interpretations of the meaning of things. This 'scholastic overkill' results in three losses. First, the child loses interest, because he or she becomes part of the 'program.' Second, the child never learns to think, because understandings are always imposed upon and meanings are interpreted for him. Third, the child loses the initiative to find out things for himself. The world of animals, plants, and minerals holds innate appeal and wonder for children. We hesitate to tamper with that natural curiosity, but have instead chosen to try and create a context that allows them to become naturalists before they undertake serious science study."

Make sure your education is never so formal that one day you notice something important missing in your child's eyes. A parent must never extinguish the fire. We parents must live by the words of the Irish poet, William Butler Yeats, who wrote, "Education is not the filling of a bucket, but the lighting of a fire."

16

"Come to Me, all you who labor and are heavy laden and I will give you rest. Take My yoke upon you and learn from Me, for I am gentle and lowly in heart, and you will find rest for your souls. For My yoke is easy and My burden is light." Matthew 11:28-30

JESUS SAYS "MY YOKE is easy..." Are you stressed with your children? With your husband? Do you feel like you *must* do *all* the suggestions and *every* page in the textbook or curriculum that you are using? If God has called you to homeschool, He does *not* intend for you to be stressed and burned out under this task.

God has placed a unique and special calling on the hearts of many mothers and fathers, especially during the past couple of decades. For most women homeschooling in our society today, the greatest responsibility rests on the mother because Dad is at work. As we Moms carry out our homeschooling responsibilities, God is impressing upon us that academic achievement is not His main concern. Simply stated, God's main concern is that our children end up with hearts consecrated to Him. On the other hand, if academic achievement is OUR main concern, each additional child God gives us increases the pressure to "keep up" academically, thereby pushing God's goal of "consecrated hearts" further and further away from becoming a reality.

Everyone's idea of a large family is different. Your "large family" might be 3, 4 or 5 children. Our large family has 7. In the article that follows, I hope to share some of what I have learned in the past 14 years so that you might find encouragement as you travel along your "narrow road less traveled." So get real comfy with a cup of tea and let's settle down for a long chat.

Education has affected every aspect of our lives. Charlotte Mason, who was an educator from the late 1800's stated that "Education is an Atmosphere, a Discipline, a Life." I have found this to be true and have discovered that 'school' is not something that happens from 9-3:00 each day. Because of the atmosphere we have purposefully created in our home, education starts the minute the children's feet hit the floor in the morning and lasts until their heads hit the pillows at night. This atmosphere is designed to be a discipline, a life that establishes the quality of our relationships with one another.

At the beginning or our journey, when we were homeschooling two small children, I felt the usual pressure to place them in a pre-school program. The Lord's hand was graciously on our lives even then as I remember saying, "Why do we need to send them to pre-school when I can teach them myself!" By the time our oldest was 11, we had seven children; five six and under. I know what it is like to homeschool with a baby, toddlers, preschoolers, and all the in-betweens! Looking back, I actually miss those days filled with babies who so often fussed while we tried to read aloud. I wouldn't exchange those times for anything in the world. I have learned through the mistakes that I made while the Lord patiently directed me to take on His yoke. Now, my children range from 7 through 19, and we are still on our homeschool journey.

A FLY ON THE WALL

I always wanted 'to be a fly on the wall' of another homeschooling family. My home was sometimes noisy, chaotic, and the wiggles never seemed to completely make their way out of their little bodies. I was once at a friend's house who homeschooled her 5 children (ages 4 to 10). Her house was absolutely quiet while her children did school in their various bedrooms. I was convinced that something was wrong with me. Whenever someone drops by our house unexpectedly, my children all crowd around the front door and we probably looked ridiculous, all eight of us, hanging out the door to welcome our guest! Just come on over for a virtual visit as I share with you a typical day in our house and how we got where we are.

GOD IS IMPRESSING UPON US THAT ACADEMIC ACHIEVEMENT IS NOT HIS MAIN CONCERN.

OUR TYPICAL DAY

Our day starts at 6:30 AM when my oldest daughter (who is 17) starts to play the piano. I like to get up earlier than the children. Hopefully, by that time I am refreshed in the Lord and ready for them. My children have all chosen to read their Bibles. They do this while my daughter practices, so the house stays relatively quiet during this time (except when my 7 year old bounds down the stairs singing, talking, *any*thing to catch everyone's attention). He is not reading yet, so he sits on my lap while I read to him from the Psalms or read a Bible story. Although, two of my children learned to read with little effort at age five or before, the other five children were not ready to read until 7, 8, or almost nine. I know that reading aloud to my son will develop his reading readiness and I am not concerned that he was not reading by age six.

A word about delayed learning: When I read the books written by Dr. Raymond and Dorothy Moore, I realized I needed to slow down. In the book, *Better Late Than Early,* the Moores state, "Rather sharp developmental differences appear between boys and girls during the early years. Nearly all of us have sat in schoolrooms where girls were generally considered to be brighter than boys." And..."Girls simply mature faster than boys. During the early years, girls are commonly six to nine months or more ahead of boys in maturity. So they are more nearly ready for school. Their superior early achievement is one of the clearest proofs of the importance of readiness in school." The Moores have advocated homeschooling for over 50 years. They have encouraged a relaxed approach to homeschooling with sound research as to why institutionalized education is not working. My frustration is that, even though I intuitively understand the need to be a relaxed homeschooler, I still tend to stray back to a traditional educational mind set.

MORE OF OUR TYPICAL DAY | SUNS UP! CHORES DONE?

In her wonderful set of booklets entitled *Wisdom's Way of Learning,* Marilyn Howshall says, "When training children in chores, try to view the tasks not just as something that needs to get done, but keep a mind set of training their character in responsibility, and training their hearts toward self-initiated service toward you and the household. Repetition with your instruction over the years will yield the bountiful fruit of helpful, unselfish children who are a blessing to you and to others." (*Develop a Lifestyle Routine* by Marilyn Howshall, p.12).

Our list of Lifetime Learning Chores |

- ◻ Develop regular responsibility
- ◻ Contribute significance to the household
- ◻ Teach volunteer service to others beginning within the family
- ◻ Provide raw material for real-life booklets

When the piano stops all the children scramble to start their chores, glad that it's time to make the vacuum cleaner roar, fold the two loads of clothes generated daily, bring in firewood, and whatever other tasks are necessary for keeping a family of nine running smoothly. Chores are such a wonderful way to teach the character we desire our children to have. 'School' is not just the academics, but involves everything that happens in our day. It is a Lifestyle of Learning as each aspect of the day brings opportunity to train our children to love one another, be diligent, cheerful, and to glorify God in all that we do.

My oldest son cared for our chickens and ducks until he started to work full time a year ago. Through this responsibility he developed a strong interest in poultry and studied many aspects of their care. He also raised and cared for our family dog and even took a class to train it. Now his younger brother cares for the chickens, ducks, and dog and has taken it upon himself to learn what is necessary to care for them.

Taking care of animals has created an interest in our children in the heart warming animal stories of James Herriot. We also have a small rabbitry where we raise Jersey Wooly and Mini Rex Rabbits. We show and breed our rabbits and several of my children have a Rabbit Notebook which includes every topic imaginable. So, you can see that what started out just as a chore has become a delight directed family learning experience where we have read books both together and independently, and have used the internet to research answers to whatever questions we might have. Animals also provide a wonderful means to develop godly character in our children.

Now that my youngest is 7, my days are likely to flow more smoothly than they did when five of my children were little. From the moment the children are up they are learning! Once everyone is dressed and ready for the day, we complete our chores before breakfast. As I have said, chores (just as much as academics) are part of the learning that prepares our children for life. This part of the day should not be neglected as it will give fruit as your children mature if you are diligent while they are small. It is a time in which character is taught through the daily tasks that must be accomplished in the home. They will learn diligence, the ability to stay with a task until it is done, thoroughness in completing the task, not to mention working well with others. This last trait is important because it relates to how we learn to love one another. For me, this is a real biggie.

Children tend to magnify the shortcomings of their parents because of the principle "more is caught than taught." That is why it is important that I learn to truly know Him because without *love*, I am *nothing*!

I Corinthians 13. To me, my home is a reflection of who I am in Christ. When I was single and on my own I discovered that I could not learn in a disorderly environment. This has also been true for my children. When I was a newlywed, I knew very little about the skills necessary for keeping a home. So, from the time my children were small I have included them in such daily chores as cooking, cleaning, animal husbandry, and gardening. My goal has been to give them the necessary skills so that they will not have to go through years of learning these things once they are on their own.

Again: "When training children in chores, try to view the tasks not just as something that needs to get done, but keep a mind set of training their character in responsibility, and training their heart toward self-initiated service toward you and the household. Repetition with your instruction over the years will yield the bountiful fruit of helpful, unselfish children who are a blessing to you and to others." ("Wisdom's Way of Learning" by Marilyn Howshall, p. 12).

The Son in Us for a Lifetime

During breakfast, or soon afterwards, we start our day with Bible. We often memorize passages together and I have been amazed at how my children's 'speech difficulties' are improved just as a blessing of this daily habit. We have always done this together, toddlers to teens all together. As character and obedience is something that can be taught through whatever activity the children are involved in, this also has been a time for training the younger ones.

Gathering Around for Table Time

- Train the heart
- Develop discipline of habit
- Develop learning skills

Table time is the time of our day for the disciplines of writing and math. During the winter months, especially, the children start their day with copy work activities. They copy from the Bible into a Bible Notebook with the goal of someday transcribing the whole New Testament. Children learn to talk through 'copying' the conversation of adults and we have found this to be the same with written language. In my opinion, the easiest way to learn language arts is through copy work. The child can learn punctuation, grammar and usage, spelling, and the mechanics of writing through the daily use of copying good literature. I have used this method for years. My definition of "burn-out" is trying to give 5 or 6 children different spelling tests.

A Few Suggestions

▫ Learning the mechanics of grammar is best put off until a child is at least 11 or 12, thereby saving the time of trying to teach and re-teach a discipline that a child is not ready to learn.

▫ Waiting until your children are older means that it is possible for them to be taught the same skills together.

▫ It is more meaningful to learn something when the need to know it arises. Unless a child makes something his own (gains "ownership" of the knowledge) he will likely not retain it no matter how many times you teach it.

CANNED CURRICULUM VIOLATES GOD'S PURPOSES.

What About Math?

The longer I have homeschooled, the more my attitude has changed regarding how to teach math to younger children. I was not the best math student and naturally did not have confidence in my ability to teach it. We parents always want to "discover" the ultimate curriculum before we begin teaching a subject. However, in being so curriculum dependant, we often end up squelching our children's desire to learn by putting them in a formal program too soon. It has taken me so long to learn this that only my younger ones are benefitting from my newly learned perspective.

What have we used for math that has actually worked for us? I started off every one of my children with *Pre-Math It!* This is a wonderful math program, utilizing dominoes and some terrific math tricks that children never forget. I no longer depend on a traditional curriculum for math because (although these might work for you) none of them totally suited my children's individual needs or allowed them to learn mastery of concepts. Some of the children surged ahead while others needed more repetition than a curriculum offered. Following *Pre-Math It!* I found *Math It!* to be a great help in teaching those wonderful tricks of math.

I wish I could say that I teach all the children from the same math book and page, but the only time we are all in the same book and on the same page is when we read aloud! My five younger children have differing abilities, none of them being in the same "place" at the same time. One forgets how to "carry" but never on the same day as the other. One is ready to learn multiplication but another suddenly can't remember how to add (which he needed to solve the multiplication problem!). The children do their math at the same time but that is as far as it goes.

Another wonderful way to teach math is through playing! Oh, do my children ever love games. Monopoly is a favorite as well as the math game, "Muggins" . There is much more I could say about teaching math skills but the booklet, *Taking the Frustration Out of Math*, by Mary Hood, will give you more in formation and encouragement which might fit your family situation.

A Lifetime of Reading 'Real Books'

If you have even two children, homeschooling can be a challenge. The more children you have, the greater the challenge seems. Throughout the years, I have constantly tried to evaluate how I was doing. Ever so gradually the Lord helped me move away from the traditional mind set of education to an understanding of what true education really is.

> *"True Education is teaching children how to learn, equipping them to learn, and guiding them into their specific life-purpose by God's design."*
>
> *Wisdom's Way of Learning* by Marilyn Howshall

If you choose to follow the 'traditional' approach with its attendant grade levels, you will find yourself attempting to fill your child's day with "have-tos" and "shoulds". If one child is in third grade and the other is in first, your day might seem never-ending! Think of me with seven! I would be teaching around 40 different subjects on various levels. I would be burned out, irritable, striving (and I mean striving) for excellence and not finding the rest because *my* yoke is not *His* yoke, and *my* yoke is surely not going to be easy! When you homeschool with a traditional text or workbook approach, the education is canned, isolating the children (whether in the same room or not) into separate learning units. It is difficult to keep up with what the children are learning as one of them might be studying plants and another the human body. Your job is then reduced to correcting the workbooks (which creates the need for tedious testing), scoring , and grading of work. I tried this one year and I wasted valuable time that I could have spent with my family living life and doing 'real' things.

> *"Canned curriculum violates God's purpose. Scholarship should be individual and creative through a process of learning that produces a delight-directed student, a student who knows how to learn and will pursue the development of his God-given abilities. You will not reap the fruit of individuality in your children if you clone their education. This approach to child-rearing and home-schooling will suffocate our children's individual purposes. Violation of this principle will result in settling for a generic education, one that does not prepare an individual for life according to God's design."*
>
> *Wisdom's Way Of Learning* by Marilyn Howshall

I have found that in our home the easiest approach to homeschooling is one which is more relaxed. I realize that each home is different and the needs of each family and child varies since God has a unique destiny for each individual. But, our job as parents is to guide our children so that we and they can identify what calling God has for their lives. I am sharing what we have found to work for us.

TEACHING THE SUBJECTS

Rather than have each of my children pursue a subject from different textbooks, (and on different grade levels where I would find it impossible to completely know and involve myself in what they are learning), we approach most of the different subjects together. This is one way that God has made my yoke easy. We begin with what my oldest two are learning and my younger ones simply learn the same thing at the same time. After all, if you take a certain subject and look at the typical, graded, textbook for each grade in that subject, you will notice that rarely do all the textbooks cover the same topic at the same time in the different grades. In fact, the year we used the traditional textbook approach I noticed that each child was studying something different even though we were all studying, say, history. That was too much work!

So, instead, we decided to all use one textbook for history or science and I read it aloud to all of my children. For most subjects, this worked well since there was a unity in our learning and much time saved. Another reason I didn't like the textbook approach is that my children did not have to develop critical thinking skills because the answers they were searching for were provided for them, in bold print, in the form of multiple choice questions. I also found that any decent book, even one from the children's section of the library, had more detail on a given subject than most of the textbooks offered to home-schoolers. Textbooks are little better than a general survey of a subject; or, at best, little more than a Christian encyclopedia.

What I have found works best in the education of our children, and with the least amount of stress for our family, is to do unit studies. For years, I used a popular unit study curriculum put out by another homeschool mom. I have always been drawn to the unit study approach for our family. For six years I purchased a prepackaged unit study curriculum only because I feared doing "my own thing." Curricula which is written by one homeschool mom for her children becomes generic when you try to use it with your family. Following the Holy Spirit's leading for our family turned out to be the easiest way to go for me. Looking back, I was as much in to the prepackaged unit study as I would have been into any textbook curricula. It is possible to teach your children in a non-traditional way, yet still force-feed them in the same way as you were taught in the public school system. I think it takes time (in my case years) for us to be renewed in mind and for the Spirit to correct our thinking of what education really is. At this point we no longer use a 'canned' unit curriculum but one that I make up myself simply by choosing 'Real Books' to read aloud or that a child can read independently as part of the unit we are studying. According to Raymond Moore, children of the same age may be as much as 4 or 5 years apart in individual ability. Why, as homeschoolers, do we think we must imitate a system that doesn't work *and* causes division within our own family?

Recently our family was learning about the Lewis and Clark Expedition. We read aloud some 'real books' which met the interest of the varying levels of my children. My oldest daughter also read independently one of the books on Sacajewea that would not have interested the others. The boys became Lewis, or Clark, or a river man, while the dog became 'Seaman' (the dog on the actual expedition). The two younger girls took turns being Sacajewea. They read about it, wrote about it for their History Notebooks, and learned about some of the plant and animal life along our own river just like Lewis and Clark did along the rivers they traveled.

When teaching many children, learning about history together is enough to give the unity you are looking for. It provides cohesiveness while peaking the children's interests in a given subject. It was because of a unit study on birds that my oldest daughter (9 or 10 at the time) acquired a lifelong passion for learning about birds. Her unit study has never ended! Several years ago, when we were studying creation, my son (around 13 at the time) devoured the books I had chosen to read aloud before we got around to reading them as a family.

My children have enough ways to express themselves individually within their Notebooks, through copy work of passages of literature, poems, related magazine pictures, and their own artwork. Each of the pages added to their Notebook is placed into a plastic sheet protector. It gives their work a finished, professional look that they can be proud to show their friends or family.

PRODUCTIVE FREE TIME
Learning to be Productive, Learning as a Passion
In the afternoons, while my youngest daughter practices the piano, the others read a book of their own choosing. Often, I find them reading again one of the books we already read aloud! Each of my children also has other notebooks in the areas of their own personal interest. In an institutional school setting (which is often replicated by homeschooling parents) children produce piles of paperwork from their workbooks. Instead, my children have each made Notebooks which express their interests and what they have learned. They all

have a Bible Notebook, History Notebook, and a Nature Notebook. Examples of other Notebooks which some of the children have created are Notebooks on birds, trains, butterflies, horses, drawing, rabbits, and poultry. During Notebook Time they might choose to research and add to the pages in one of these books.

A couple of my daughters are learning to sew, crotchet, and do other crafts. The boys may do legos, tinker toys, Fischertechnique, or make a very creative setup for their cars. We may go on a Nature Walk down to the river at the bottom of our road. There we might see wild flowers, trees, rocks, wildlife, insects, turtles, birds, and so much more. I love the book, The Handbook of Nature Study, by Anna Botsford Comstock, as it contains endless ideas for nature study and lots of information to answer children's curiosity. Of course *all* the children keep frequent entries in their Nature Notebook with enthusiasm! We're hooked on the art of Notebooking!

Now It's Sundown

As the day ends, it is time for making supper. And, another chance to learn! So we get out the cookbooks and *everyone* helps make supper. Does learning ever end? I hope not! Soon Dad drives in the driveway in his green Ford Pickup truck and is greeted by happy children telling about their adventures in the woods down by the river or what they saw right in the woods in back of the house. Ahhhh . . . school is done!! As Mom checks supper on the stove, the aroma of homemade muffins drifts through the air as the girls mix up a delicious salad, sometimes with homemade dressing. The younger children chatter with Dad, telling him about the Ruby Throated Hummingbird that came to the feeder today, and how the Titmouse stole some hair from the dog for a nest, and about the wild rabbit that scurried across the yard this morning, and how cute one of the bunnies was when it stood on it's hind legs for a treat. On and on the chatter goes.

A little later, the family is complete as the oldest son returns home from a day driving a concrete truck. The conversations get louder as father and son talk about their day. Technical talk of corporate jet airplanes and current events around the world is discussed around the table as everyone gathers together to continue a tradition absent in most homes today. Dad livens the home with his conversation and explains how a tornado develops or how a machine works. Often he points out something on the globe or map as the children eagerly gather around. Such an exciting teacher. Is 'school' ever really done?

Finally, the family gathers together in the living room and Dad reads from the Bible. We all pray for relatives or missionaries, some close by, others scattered far away. If we aren't exhausted, a missionary biography is read before bed. From Sunup to Sundown...a Lifestyle Of Learning never ends! "*With only the raw material of our fragmented lives to work with, we attempt to implement new godly family desires and goals into our existing lifestyles and systems. In so doing, we create additional problems for ourselves, among them confusion and burn-out! We use the world's methods to produce something they were not designed to produce. When we finally accept the truth that the old familiar way will not produce the results we want, we are ready to receive the suggestion of a new way. Now we are ready to learn. That is what Lifestyle of Learning is all about: a new way of life, a new system applying principles instead of following programs and a fresh beginning for the entire family. ....Seek God in your homeschool. His burden is easy, His yoke is light."*

Wisdom's Way of Learning by Marilyn Howshall

Judith Kowles, the author of the article "From Sunup to Sundown," is a mother of 7 wonderful children and has been educating them at home for 20 years. She is the co-moderator of the Elijah Counsel discussion board with over 2000 members.

17

THE DAY HOMESCHOOLING DIES

MY SONS NEVER WENT to school. This past summer, my oldest son and I were discussing his upbringing, I had a realization about this movement we all call "homeschooling," and I said to Seth, "When you have kids, they will not be public schooled. They won't be private schooled. They won't be Christian schooled."

"And," I concluded, "your kids won't be home schooled, either."

The realization I had while talking with Seth is that God had begun something twenty years ago that came to be called "homeschooling," but which really wasn't about schooling at all.

THE COLLAPSE OF THE FAMILY

For thousands of years children have grown up in what today would be considered an unusual place their own homes. In this setting, parents never thought of themselves as "home schoolers." There was no alternative to children spending their days at home, having knowledge, experiences and character passed to them by their parents and extended family. What children needed to know, they learned as part of their daily lives: sowing and reaping, weather, how a business works, how to treat customers (and everyone else, for that matter).

Life was education.

Throughout history, small, homogeneous groups have attempted to provide a common education for their youth, yet it wasn't until around the mid 1800's that entire nations decided to take children out of the home and "school"" them.

The mid-1800's was a cultural turning point for the American family. The Industrial Revolution began and the siren call went out for men to leave their homes and be paid a salary (something new for most men) in exchange for their labor. The possibility of being able to increase the family's standard of living was the draw that caused men to cease being patriarchs of a family enterprise and become employees.

Around this same time, another movement was taking shape: The Common (Public) School movement. The leaders of the Public School movement were, for the most part, humanists who were concerned about two things they believed endangered America's future: The continuation of what they called religious superstitious beliefs and the influx of illiterate immigrants seeking jobs and a better life in this country. These leaders believed that realizing their two-fold goal of ridding our society of religion and providing an education for immigrant children mandated compulsory education for every child. One state after another began passing compulsory attendance laws and children followed their fathers out the front door to attend public schools en masse.

So, as dads were leaving home with a promise of employment, children were leaving home with a promise of being made employable for the next generation. Within a very short period of time, the family unit that had been tightly held together for generations, became a set of individuals going their separate ways. To the factories went the dads. To the schools went the kids. Where Mom went is the subject of another article.

It wasn't long before people forgot what it was like to be a family with Dad as the head of a "family enterprise" and the whole family working together as co-producers. In one generation, the cultural memory of children growing up at home was forgotten. Children belonged "in school" during the most productive hours of their day, learning whatever would make them employable, becoming independent, establishing strong friendships that replaced the bonds of family. And what had been a lifestyle of learning became "book learning" as education became separated from real life.

Of course, there was always a small group of families whose children never attended public school. Typically, these were America's

---

IT WASN'T LONG BEFORE PEOPLE FORGOT WHAT IT WAS LIKE TO BE A FAMILY

---

wealthiest whose children received exclusive private educations in areas intended to prepare them for leadership in government, science and industry. Most Americans don't realize that public school was never intended to prepare leaders. It has always been intended to prepare employees. [For a fuller understanding of this subject, read John Gatto's books, *The Underground History of American Education*, *A Different Kind of Teacher*, and *Dumbing us Down*].

HOW THEN SHOULD WE SCHOOL?
In the 1950's one hundred years after the public school movement began some middle class parents began to desire an educational experience for their children whose curricula was more individualized. It was

at this time that the private school movement began. I attended one of these schools in what should have been my fourth grade. It was little more than an experimental school run by one man who was also the only teacher. He didn't like having one fourth grader, so I was skipped to fifth grade where there was one other student. I don't remember learning much, but it was more fun than public school!

During the Civil Rights years, the Christian school movement began along with its own particular brand of curricula which was mainly "Christianized" public school material. The concept remained that children were to be brought out of their homes and taught by educators, (presumably Christian), who, because they were "professionals" would do a better job of training children than could the children's parents. It seemed that parents would now get the best of both worlds: a public-style education that was also Christian.

Then, in the late 1970's and early 1980's, a new schooling movement began. All over the country, parents began keeping their children home instead of sending them to one of the other schooling options. Some parents made this decision out of concern for their children's safety. Others didn't like the education their children were receiving. However, the majority decided to keep their children home simply because they wanted a relationship with them and parents didn't think this could happen very well if the kids were gone all day long. It was quite a novel (and controversial) idea that children should be kept home during the schooling hours of the day.

Today, parents have several choices as to how to educate their children:
- ▣ Public School
- ▣ Private School
- ▣ Christian School
- ▣ Home School

Note that the above choices relate to *where* the child is educated.

In the past 150 years we have changed the first word, but we have not changed the last word, "School." Each choice still emphasizes the fact that children are to be "schooled."

A MISUNDERSTOOD MOVEMENT?

I don't know how keeping our children home during the day came to be known as "Home Schooling," but I do have a theory: If I asked most adults, "What is the most appropriate activity for children, age six to age eighteen, during the days Monday through Friday?" Most adults would say, "These are the years when a child is being schooled, of course." That is why we have such phrases in our vocabulary as the "school age child." So, if a child is to be "schooled" during these formative years, the only real question is, "*Where* will he be schooled?" Today, the answer is, "He will either be public schooled, private schooled, Christian schooled, or home schooled." Assuming, then, that every child is to "be schooled" during the day, if he is home during the day, he will be *home* schooled during the day. Hence the origin of the label "homeschooling."

CHALLENGING A BELIEF

Is "schooling" really supposed to be a child's primary daily activity? It wasn't until the advent of the modern public school movement. Schooling a child was never meant to be the "constant" with the variable being *where* the child spends his or her day. It has always been just the other way around.

What is so problematic with the term "Home Schooling" is what it has done to parents whose children are spending their days at home. Giving an activity a label means something to those involved in the activity. If we are comfortable with certain words in the label and not so comfortable with other words, those words with which we feel least secure will take on greater significance. Insecurity is a nice word for fear. Whatever we fear becomes a driver in our lives as we attempt to overcome our fear and feel secure again.

When we sent our children to school, we felt a sense of security that trained professionals were educating them. We didn't pretend that we could do a job which others had spent years being trained to do. We might feel that we could raise our children in some areas, but we certainly could not provide for their education.

Then, one day, we became homeschoolers. Insecure homeschooler; but homeschoolers, nevertheless. However, since what we were doing was labeled "homeschooling," we, in our insecurity, actually became home-SCHOOLERS rather than HOME-schoolers. The importance of our children becoming educated (isn't that what children do during the day?) took on greater prominence than the importance of them being home. This is understandable when we realize that there is no cultural memory of what having our children home really means to the family or to society.

What did I mean when I told my son, "And, your kids won't be homeschooled"? During Seth's years at home, his academic education was never the main priority. In our home, we did have a rigid priority structure, but those priorities were first, relationships; second, practical skills; and, finally, academics. Seth grew up with a strong academic upbringing, but academics were never our priority. Seth is a skilled, very competent individual of the highest character. He is also one of the happiest young men I have ever known. As I look back at Seth's time at home, I have come to realize that he was never "homeschooled." He simply grew up in a most unusual place—his own home.

When our children were young we would take them with us to the store. Other kids were in school. The check-out lady would inevitably ask, "You boys aren't in school today?" Since the boys knew we were homeschoolers, they would respond, "No, ma'am, we're homeschooled."

STARTING OVER

If I could do it all over again, I would not call ourselves "homeschool-ers." I have actually come to dislike the term because I think it creates significant problems. If I were starting over again, when the lady at the store says, "You boys aren't in school today?" I would teach the boys to say, simply, "No ma'am," and let it go at that.

In just the past year I have noticed a growing distinction between families who are homeschooling and those whose children are home, but not being home-SCHOOLED. Are the "not-being-homeschooled" children receiving a quality upbringing, including a quality education? Today enough research exists that I can honestly say an unequivocal yes! I would even go so far as to say that the not-being-homeschooled child is receiving an education which is superior to the child being homeschooled.

The availability of what has come to be known as prepackaged curricula is helping manifest a separation of the two types of families who were once grouped together under the one term: homeschool-ers. Many parents purchase prepackaged curricula because they don't understand what God originally intended when He began this move-ment over twenty years ago.

What do you think your children should be doing all day now that they are home? Probably the most obvious way to determine what you really believe is to ask yourself, "Is my child the constant or is my child's academic education the constant?" Look at the materials you use to bring learning into your child's life. Do you use graded, pre-packaged, curricula? Is your child in a grade as he would be if he were in an institutional setting? Do you follow the institutionalized Scope & Sequence educational model? Or, have you stepped completely out of the lock-step, institutional way of raising your child?

This article is not intended to discourage, but to give hope. In most parents' hearts is the desire to reprioritize their lives around what is truly important to them: having a relationship with their children. To bring your children home can be an immense lifestyle change. For some, making this change has to be done in stages. If you have brought your children home it may have been necessary (for a season) to place before them the ever popular curriculum-in-a-box. Hopefully, that season will be short. Our children never went to school, were never in a grade, and we never used a prepackaged curriculum.

Nevertheless, it took us a while to learn all that I am sharing with you here. Be encouraged. You are allowed to do what your heart tells you is right.

IF WE AREN'T HOMESCHOOLING, THEN WHAT ARE WE DOING?
Right now, nearly two million children are spending their days at home rather than at school. They are beginning to bring to a close a 150 year detour which began in the 1850's and which seriously harmed family life and Kingdom community as God initially intended them to be lived. Families are returning to that road whose name is Life As It Was Intended To Be. Along this road we can see a different possibility for each individual child: Not just employment, but entrepreneurship. Not just college, but collaboration. Not just a career, but creating things never before seen or even considered.

Allow me to offer some suggestions:

▫ Don't send your children to school. Any school. Bring them home. Raise them to be the individuals God has created them to become.

▫ Don't bring the school, any school (along with its efficient, but arbitrary, grade levels, scope & sequence, and boxed curricula) into your home. Allow your children to learn through life and the relationships around them.

▣ Learn how to awaken curiosity in your children.

▣ The only thing that should be prepackaged is your child. By this I mean your child was born with all the talents, giftings, and callings put into him or her since the foundation of the world. Find out what these are and let your child become truly good at what you find.

▣ Dad's heart must turn toward his children and the hearts of the children must turn toward Dad. Ultimately, this may bring Dad out of the corporate workforce to come home. This final step may take another generation to be fulfilled. But, for it to be fulfilled, Dads must at least begin moving in that direction (ie. Giving his children the option of becoming entrepreneurs).

▣ In your own home, let homeschooling die. In other words, don't homeschool your children. God has asked us to raise a generation prepared for the future by becoming exactly what He intended each person to become. This will be different for each and every child. Your home is the place where the acorn can become the oak tree. Or, the seed can become the maple tree. Or, the other seed can become the pine tree. Plant your children squarely in their own home and allow the individual God created to grow.

18

SPRING SEEMS TO BE the hardest time of all for home schoolers. Winter weather has kept us inside, but now that spring has come we've got too much to do to enjoy the pretty weather. The drudgery of routine has set in; work has piled up; and we've had a chance to fail miserably at reaching goals that seemed so easy to achieve when we started schooling in the fall. Add to that level of stress a series of small crises, and you have a recipe for homeschool burnout.

Gail Felker, in *Homeschooling Today* magazine, says homeschool burnout is a condition in which "the teaching parent is anxious, depressed, discouraged, overwhelmed, and ready to quit. Burnout is not uncommon. Special-needs schools, churches, and nursing homes, for example, have a large employee turnover due to burnout. Demanding, people-oriented professions are most at risk. For the home-schooler, it often results in sending the children back to public school."

BURNOUT AND THE 80/20 PRINCIPLE

One of the most cherished tenets of business is the "80/20 Principle." This scientifically proven principle says there is always an imbalance between causes and results, inputs and outputs, and effort and reward, and that imbalance generally assumes the proportions of 20% to 80%. In other words, 80 percent of the results you want to see will come from 20 percent of your effort. In business, this means that 80% of your sales will come from 20% of your products; 80% of the important work will be done by 20% of your employees; 80% of the actual benefits of a project will be developed in only 20% of the time spent on the project, and so on. So the key to good business management is to find the 20% that is most productive and enhance it, and to find the 80% that is not productive and figure out ways to either eliminate it or make it part of the 20%.

The 80/20 Principle applies to other areas of life as well. For example, good students innately know that 80% of an exam usually covers only 20% of the topics from the course, and they have discovered how to find out which 20% of the material to study to make an 80 or higher on the exam. The 80/20 Principle even works relationally. 80% of the value of your relationships usually comes from only 20% of the people you know.

OK, so what does this have to do with "Homeschool Burnout?" First, we need to understand that a major cause of burnout is the feeling of being overwhelmed and under-supported. Here are some common ways this feeling is verbalized:

- This isn't fun anymore (in fact, it's a real drag).
- I feel like things are spinning out of control.
- There's not enough me to go around.
- My life is fragmented (pulled in too many directions, torn into too many pieces).
- I feel like I'm trying to keep too many balls up in the air (or spin too many plates).
- I'm drowning.
- There's too much to do and not enough time to do it.

- There's too much to do and I'm expected to do it all myself.
- I don't feel anything but anger (frustration, irritation) or sadness (grief, depression, sorrow).
- I resent having to be responsible for everything.
- I am the one who has to pick up everything that "falls through the cracks."
- I am constantly disappointed.

Here are some common ways this feeling expresses itself physically: [1] a tightness in the throat, chest or between the shoulder blades, [2] pain in the lower back, [3] headaches or dizziness, [4] chronic fatigue, [5] numbness of certain parts of the body, [6] anxiety and tenseness, [7[difficulty swallowing, [8] nausea, [9] upset stomach or irritable bowel, [10] ringing in the ears.

Any and all of the above verbalizations and physical symptoms are a good indication that we are bogged down in the 80% of our lives that is non-productive and that undermine our sense of well-being. The good news about the 80/20 Principle is that there are a very few, key activities that will dramatically improve our happiness and sense of productivity. What do I mean by "key activities?" Well, do you know the simple, key activities that distinguish thin people from people who struggle with their weight? If you ever went to a "Weigh Down" workshop, you know that thin people don't munch, they eat only when they are hungry, they stop eating when they are full, and they eat smaller portions of food. In contrast, people who struggle with their weight tend to be "grazers" who eat large portions of food and don't stop eating even when they feel stuffed. This means that becoming thin doesn't necessarily require a massive amount of will power counting calories, weighing portions, and developing meal plans. The average person can lose weight by sticking to the key activities of eating less and becoming aware of when they are hungry and when they are full.

What are the simple, key activities that distinguish financially stable people from people with chronic financial troubles? Financially stable people resist going into debt, they save, and they don't fill their lives with expensive doodads. So what does this mean? This means that becoming financially stable doesn't necessarily require keeping track of every expenditure to the penny, becoming a Scrooge, and denying yourself your dreams. The average person can become financially stable by following a few, key principles of money management.

Now, back to the 80/20 Principle. The book, *80/20 Principle* says, There are always a few key inputs to what happens and they are often not the obvious ones. If the key causes can be identified and isolated, we can very often exert more influence on them than we think possible. What this means is that there are a few key things that cause us to feel overwhelmed and under-supported, that contribute to that feeling of always being on edge and the tenseness in our bodies, and that make us want to throw up our hands and quit.

SIMPLE MEASURES

OK, what are some simple measures we can take? First of all, we can identify our "energy vampires." These are the people, activities, and beliefs that literally "suck" the energy and enthusiasm out of us.

People as Energy Vampires

Not only can groups be draining, but certain individuals can cost us a lot of energy. In our former church, there was a woman who was like a huge emotional vacuum. Her neediness and negativity would suck all of the optimism and energy out of me. I had to learn to let someone else try to help her.

When I first started homeschooling three boys, I tried to keep up with women's Bible studies, homeschooling field trips and other get-togethers, but it didn't take long to realize these social outings didn't provide me with enthusiasm, they only wore me down.

I didn't just work a 40 hour week, I was on the job 24/7.

I also had to learn to say no. It's amazing that people will assume since you're home all day, you're available. They wouldn't dream of calling a career woman at her office and asking her to take the afternoon off to listen to their problems, but they will call you and assume you're free to help them. I learned to think of myself as a "career woman," only my career was managing a home and educating my children. I didn't just work a 40 hour week, I was on the job 24/7, so didn't have to apologize or lie when I said, "I'm committed this afternoon."

Before you know it, you can spend 80% of your time on social activities that have a pay-back of less than 20% in terms of what is really important to you. There are two key solutions to the "People as Energy Vampires" problem. (1) Pare down your involvement to only those 20% of social activities that have real meaning to you, and (2) Get an answer-phone and let it take all calls for certain hours each day. If your household is like mine, just leaving an answer-phone on most of the day saves me about 45 minutes in answering telemarketing calls.

Activities as Energy Vampires

One of the best pieces of stress-reducing advice I ever got was from a time management book. It said to mentally visualize myself going through a typical day. This meant visualizing getting out of bed, getting dressed, fixing breakfast, brushing my teeth, and so on...every little activity I typically did in a day. As I screened through my day, the book said to notice any time I felt irritation, tension, or resistance, and jot down that activity.

What an eye-opener! The first thing I realized is that it irritates me to be interrupted while I am in the bathroom. Sounds pretty stupid, right? But what this meant was that I was starting every day irritated because there was hardly ever a time I wouldn't be interrupted while I was in the bathroom. Stupid problem. Simple solution to eliminating that source of irritation: Always close the door when I go into the bathroom and tell everyone that when the bathroom door is closed I am not to be disturbed.

By the time I finished visually screening a typical day, I realized that there were dozens of annoyances like the bathroom scenario. None of them was significant enough by itself to ruin my day, but a day filled with 40 or 50 unconsciously irritating moments might have something to do with my being frazzled by suppertime.

Certain routine activities are always accompanied by some amount of emotional or physical pressure. What are your stressful activities? The laundry? Cooking? Shopping? I've never particularly liked to cook. Plus, taking a car-load of small boys to the grocery store has got to be on my list of "Top 10 Ways to Torture a Tired Mother." So I had to experiment with getting the grocery shopping done without wearing me out (or freaking me out when I saw the receipt), and with developing some simple menu plans that didn't exhaust me after a long day. Plus, I had to be realistic about my limitations. As much as I might want to provide my family with three, lovingly created, nutritious, home-cooked meals a day, it would be psychotic of me to think I could pull it off and still do everything else I needed to get done. So in my household, we have meals where everyone is on their own to fix something for themselves, meals that another family member prepares, and meals that I prepare, depending on everyone's schedule and what will give us the most family time around the table.

Another thing that can be done is to go through each room of the house and note anything that is irritating. Rooms have a powerful effect on our sense of well-being. They can make us feel like prisoners in our own homes or make us feel gracious and relaxed. Are there certain colors that make you feel tense? That make you feel relaxed? Could the room be re-arranged so that the pattern of traffic flow is better? Could simple changes be made that contribute to a sense of peace and order?

Do the tools you have enhance your productivity? For example, I started out writing our catalogs on an old IBM electric typewriter ($25, second-hand), made photocopied reductions of the book covers, and had to cut and paste everything together. It was a massive, time-consuming, mess-producing job. So, guess how I began to feel about the catalog? I dreaded the thought of starting each new one, and the whole time I worked on one I was a witch. It was like trying to build a modern house with stone tools. Then one day I heard Mary Pride say she always tried to invest in things that increased her productivity. I began to look around at all of the equipment I relied on. Everything from my vacuum cleaner to my typewriter was out-dated and difficult to use. So I began systematically replacing my "tools," starting with the equipment I used most and that caused me the most aggravation. I also began investing in skills that made me more productive. I learned how to use word processing programs and scanners and Adobe Photoshop. I read every household and time management book I could get my hands on. I tried to increase my knowledge and skill in every area that drained energy.

Another stressful area for home schooling parents is the "schooling" itself. In our desire to make sure we don't leave any educational gaps, we tend to overdo. We need to evaluate our homeschools by the 80/20 Principle. What are the key areas we need to be concentrating on? How can we eliminate the unnecessary and ineffectual? What simple changes can we make to decrease stress and enhance enthusiasm?

Lifestyle as an Energy Vampire

An article in *U.S. News and World Report* focused on sleep-deprivation in America. Because of our fast-paced lifestyles, very few Americans ever know the clarity of thought and level of energy that comes with being fully rested. Not only do adults suffer from lack of sleep, but now children are at risk for sleep deprivation, because their lives have become as demanding as their parents'.

Although this seems elementary, the amount of rest you get and the kind of food you eat can have a dramatic effect on your ability to cope with life's demands. Some questions you might ask yourself are: What makes me happy? What energizes me? What makes me feel productive? What comforts and renews me when I feel worn out and used up? What am I passionate about?

You can make major lifestyle changes that refresh you, or you can make minor changes by building "happiness islands" into your day. For example, I am a person who needs solitude in order to recharge and reconnect with what is important to me. Yet for years I lived in a four room house with three active boys and five or six employees coming in and out of an upstairs office all day. It was a radical invasion of my privacy, and some days I thought I would lose my mind. I had to force myself to find reflective time, to create "happiness islands" for myself. Sometimes these "happiness islands" were as simple as taking a walk by myself, or shutting myself in my bedroom with a good book. Sometimes they had to be more extreme, like flying to Dallas to participate in a horse-judging seminar, or taking the boys to the beach for a few days by ourselves. In the process, I found out which colors, smells, sights, and activities renew me.

Beliefs as Energy Vampires

Think about it. Here we are, absolute amateurs, sitting around our kitchen tables, using our own children as guinea pigs and clinging to a belief that we can somehow give them a better education than an American institution that has multi-million dollar facilities and a professional staff, and that spends an average of $5,500 a year on each child. The only tools we have at our disposal are our own willingness to give it a try and assorted teaching materials modeled after those used in the public schools. So we are surrounded with constant questions questions from our relatives, our friends, members of our church that undermine our convictions. Even worse, we have to battle questions from our own minds like "Can I really pull this off? Do I know what I'm doing? Am I doing too much or too little? Am I using the right teaching material? Am I simply wasting time? Am I going to warp my children and make them total misfits?" No wonder we struggle with burnout!

Obviously, these questions can become "energy vampires" that erode our sense of confidence about what we are trying to accomplish. We need to surround ourselves with confidence builders that reinforce our convictions, like books by John Gatto that let us know all is not as great as it may seem in the public schools. Or books by Raymond Moore that tell us that warm, loving, family life overcomes any deficiencies there may be in our teaching materials and methods. Or books by Edith Schaeffer that make us realize our homes have the power to mold lives in eternal ways.

There are three major "energy vampire" beliefs I have noticed as

I've talked with home schooling families across the nation. You can probably spot more self-defeating beliefs in your own life, but here are three I have noticed:

The belief in scarcity

This is the belief in "not enough" not enough time, energy, money, opportunities, resources, and so on. When we hold a belief in scarcity, we limit ourselves. We tend to not step outside of our own "boxes," because we feel we must hoard what little we have and we feel that no matter how much we try, our efforts won't be "enough." We are always afraid we are going to "run out" of time, energy, money, opportunities, etc., etc. When we choose to believe in scarcity, we not only limit ourselves, but we insult God—the God Who is Enough, and Who, in fact, promises to give to us exceeding abundantly, pressed down, and running over. We also lock ourselves into anxiety over finances and time pressure, and into regret and grief over wasted time, energy, and money. One of the reasons our family has tried to keep Hudson Taylor's biography in print is that he was a man with a firm conviction that "God would always be enough," and his response to every extremity was, "Now we have an opportunity to see what God can do!'"

The belief in difficulty

The word "bummer" has become firmly entrenched in the American vocabulary. It is reflective of a widely held belief that life is a hassle, a battle, an uphill climb, a constant proof of Murphy's Law (everything that can go wrong will'"). Yes, it is true, we live in a fallen world, but that doesn't mean we have to approach everything with a What's the use?'" attitude. One of the most important lessons I ever learned was about the power of repetition. I used to never make up my bed, because

I would hit the floor running each morning and never slow down until I fell into bed again at night. The unmade bed always bothered me, but it seemed like an insurmountable task to tackle first thing in the morning. A friend happened to mention that if you do something for six months, it becomes a habit and it no longer requires any extra emotional or physical energy. Silly as it may sound, I thought, "Maybe I can

---

WHEN WE CHOOSE TO BELIEVE IN SCARCITY, WE NOT ONLY LIMIT OURSELVES, BUT WE INSULT GOD—THE GOD WHO IS ENOUGH.

---

try making up my bed for six months." Well, that was twenty five years ago, and I don't even think about making up the bed anymore. I just do it when I get up. Since that time, I have used the power of repetition to eliminate the draining effect of certain tasks that I dislike. I've found out that social scientists call this "unconscious competence." All tasks, particularly tasks that require overcoming a certain amount of inner resistance, have a "competency curve" where once you reach a level of mastery, no further mental, emotional or physical effort is required. We see this all the time when we teach a child to read. For months it seems like we are getting nowhere, but all of a sudden our child reads effortlessly.

Speaking of the word "bummer," did you know that you can change how you feel about life by simply changing the words you use? If you find your everyday conversation filled with words like exhausted," "rushed," "overloaded," "stressed," "frustrated," "disappointed," and so on, you may want to make a conscious effort to change the words you use. Find positive (or even humorous) words to replace your "bummer" words. For example, you can say, I am achieving "warp speed" instead of saying "I'm rushed" or "I'm at critical mass" instead of "I'm overwhelmed." Not only will changing your words make you think about the labels you put on your life, but it will make those around you start listening to you again. Your family has probably tuned you out because they've heard you say the same negative things over and over.

The belief in failure

Robert Kiyosaki says the most damaging beliefs the public school system teaches are (1) that mistakes are bad and (2) that there is only one right way to do something. These beliefs create a fear of failure, a fear of making mistakes, that thwart true learning. Kiyosaki further says that most true learning comes from making mistakes, from falling down and trying again like you do when you learn to walk or learn to ride a bicycle. So failure always has something to teach us, and often teaches us more than success does. Kiyosaki says there are no failures, only "outcomes" and he calls mistakes "outcomes with attached emotions."

What if we really believed God works everything for our good and even redeems our mistakes? That would dispel a lot of our fear and anxiety.

The belief that it will always be this way

One of my mother's favorite phrases is "This too, shall pass." It is her way of acknowledging the inevitability of change. Sure, right now you are up to your elbows in baby doody, your house is a wreck, and there is no way you will have supper on the table in time. No wonder you feel stressed and harbor thoughts of sending the kids to military school! But believe me, there will be a day when you would give anything to have a peanut-butter and jelly smudged four-year-old son crawl onto your lap and ask you to read *Mike Mulligan and His Steam Shovel* for the four hundredth time. These days with your children will pass you by in an instant. All of my children are now well beyond the diapers and peanut-butter stage and what I miss most are the snuggles, the little hands reaching up to me, the plaintive cries for "just one more story," the proud calls of "Mama, come quick and see what I did!" How could I ever have thought it was a hardship to read Mike Mulligan? I would gladly trade all of the clean houses in the world for more of those stressful years when my children were small and every day held a thousand new wonders for them to discover.

Beliefs have a powerful impact on how we perceive life. Next time you are frustrated, anxious, or depressed, ask yourself, "What would I have to believe to feel this way?"

Recognizing the false beliefs you allow yourself to hold about people and situations, and then consciously trying to align those beliefs with God's truth, will dramatically change the way you approach life. For example, if you believe your children are "rug rats," you will relate to them totally differently than if you believe they are blessings from God."

In *The Safest Place on Earth*, Larry Crabb says:

> "We simply do not believe in a God who is so intrinsically good that His commitment to be fully Himself is equivalent to a commitment to be very good to us. When He tells us that He is out for His own glory, and will glorify Himself by making known who He is, we can relax. It's something like a wealthy, generous father declaring his intention to display his true character. We know we're in for a bundle. That is, if were his heirs."

SPIRITUAL FRIENDSHIPS, MENTORS & CHRISTIAN COUNSELORS

We are relational beings, and, ultimately, all of our problems are relational. All of the practical areas discussed so far in this article have to do with changing how we relate to created things (like time and our living environment) and changing what we allow to affect our relationship with ourselves (our thought patterns, our energy level, etc.). But there are other relationships that contribute to stress and conflict in our lives. Yes, we may have too much to do and not enough time to do it, but this time/space problem only reaches "burn-out" when there are underlying relational problems such as tension between husband and wife, conflict between parents and children, or estrangement between fellow Christians. Usually the largest source of relational stress is in our marriages, because most of us got married without ever being taught how to make a marriage work.

Those of us with relational problems don't need time-management courses or housekeeping seminars, we need spiritual friendships, mentors, and counselors who help us develop right relationships with others and with God.

What about spiritual friendships? Unfortunately, many of us hesitate to share our deepest struggles, because we suspect other Christians will treat us like a problem that needs to be fixed. Larry Crabb says in *The Safest Place on Earth* that all Christians yearn for...

> "...a community of friends who are hungry for God, who
> knows what it means to sense the Spirit moving within them
> as they speak with you. You long for brothers and sisters who
> are intent not on figuring out how to improve your life, but
> on being with you wherever your journey leads."

We would give nearly anything to be part of a community that was profoundly safe, where people never gave up on one another, where wisdom about how to live emerged from conversation, where what is most alive in each of us is touched....where we would feel safe enough to meaningfully explore who we are with confidence so that the end point would be a joyful meeting with God.

Scripture tells us that God intends for the Body of Christ to be just that: a safe place that nourishes the godly in us and brings us to a joyful meeting with God. It is worth searching for spiritual companionship, even if we find only one or two others who befriend us spiritually.

What about mentors? Within the Body of Christ, godly older women are specifically intended to help other women be all that they can be as wives, mothers, and home-makers. But, as I once remarked to a Christian psychologist, "All of the older Christian women I know are faking it just as badly as I am!"

Most of us have struggled to become Titus 2 women keepers at home, lovers of our children and husband, etc. but very few of us have had godly older women to show us the way. Instead, we have been nurtured and discipled by women who are as unskilled as we are at fulfilling the Titus 2 mandate. I have always thought of my generation as a sandwich generation. We are sandwiched between a generation that never mentored us, and a generation that desperately needs for us to mentor them.

How do we cope with this dilemma? First, we need to take a good, hard look at who our primary influencers are. Are these women worthy role models? Can they provide us with a pattern of beliefs and godly living as well as with practical skills that we can duplicate in our own lives? Is their influence causing us to be happier and more productive, or do we relate to them because misery loves company?

Second, we can search for women worthy of modeling. Sometimes this will mean we have to settle for second-hand modeling, by reading books or listening to tapes by women who are well-respected and generally acknowledged as worthy to instruct other women. For example, most of my role models are women I never knew personally: women like Corrie Ten Boom, Edith Schaeffer, and others whose lives will withstand scrutiny.

In addition to the lack of godly, older women, there is a dearth of mature Christian counselors. It is hard to find someone to talk to whose advice isn't mixed with pop-psychology, or who doesn't try to superimpose their agenda over your problems. What do I mean by "agenda?" It's like the old saying: "When you have a new hammer, everything looks like a nail." We've all had the experience of someone trying to make our problems fit their doctrine. If they happen to be into inner healing, then our problem becomes the "nail" to their inner healing hammer." If they happen to believe in demons, then our problem becomes the "nail" to their deliverance "hammer." Don't be ashamed to seek professional help, but when you do, check the person out as carefully as you would any other mentor. And don't let anyone ever treat you like a nail."

Sin and Unbelief in Our Lives

No discussion of frustration and stress would be complete without examining whether there is any sin or unbelief in our lives that may be contributing to our feelings of being overwhelmed and under-supported. The primary relationship that undergirds all of our other relationships is the relationship we have with God. If our relationship with God is out of balance because of sin or unbelief, all other relationships suffer and no amount of time management, household organization, self-help, spiritual friendships, mentors, or counselors will help. These measures may seem to provide temporary relief, but will never address the root problem, which is our disobedience to or lack of faith in God.

Let's look at the three most common areas of sin that cause women to be stressed-out. First, there is the area of proper discipline and training of children. When we do not nurture and "admonish" our children in the ways God requires, we are not only creating children who make our lives miserable, but more importantly, we are sinning against God. Next is the area of the husband-wife relationship. If your attitude toward your husband stinks, it will be impossible to achieve a sense of peace and order in your home no matter how hard you try. Maybe your house is a wreck because you feel it's unfair for you to have to do so much work, or you feel cheated of your potential by being a mother and home-maker. Or maybe you're caught up in some secret sin like over-eating or sexual fantasies, or whatever. No matter what sin you are in, it clouds your relationship with God, with others, and with earthly things like time and money.

The bad news about sin is that it is like a disease that weakens every part of our lives. The good news is that God freely forgives and heals us if we confess our sins and turn from them.

Unbelief is a form of sin. God has provided everything we need through many precious promises, and through the shed blood of Jesus Christ. This "everything" includes strength and vision to enjoy the privilege and endure the demands of home schooling our children and running a household. The Bible says, "The wise woman builds her house, but the foolish woman tears it down with her own hands." We are foolish women when we let our sin and unbelief tear down our houses.

REACHING GROUND ZERO WITH GOD
When you're in the midst of a crisis, when you've reached the end of your rope, when you can't seem to find the inner resources to keep going for another day, you often will reach a place of "ground zero"

with God. Ground zero is a term used to designate the immediate blast area of a nuclear bomb, and sometimes life sends "bombs" that leave you feeling like you are in nuclear winter. The nuclear winters of life are times when you must come to terms with Who God really is. So in one way these times are extreme challenges, but in another way they are "gifts" from God because they give you a true perspective of what is valuable and what is not, they show you who your real friends are, and they force you to accept God on His terms.

Here is the story of one of my "ground zero" experiences. In January, 1994, due to a freak accident, a piece of metal fractured my skull and destroyed my right eye. Just before the accident occurred, Chris had resigned from the pastorate and the lease was up on the house we were renting. This meant we had sixty days to find another place to live and another source of income. The Elijah Company at that time certainly was not capable of sustaining us financially. While I was recovering from surgery for removal of my eye, well-meaning Christians came and counseled me. Most of their counsel was variations on five themes: either (1) there must be some sin in my life for me to have been injured, or (2) I had somehow "come out from under my covering of authority" for this to have happened, or (3) I would never have been injured if Chris hadn't decided to leave the pastorate, or (4) God was teaching me a powerful lesson through this, or (5) I must be a very special person for God to have let this happen to me. All of this conflicting counsel further unraveled me emotionally and I began to feel like I would throw up if I ever heard Romans 8:28 again.

After my release from the hospital, I had to be very careful in standing, and was not supposed to lift anything or do any physical work for six weeks. The only comforting aspect of that six weeks was a tape my sister sent me with the chorus, "I'm going to walk right out of this valley, lift my hands and praise the Lord!" I don't know the name of the song, but I played it over and over.

But a remarkable thing happened. Some people I had thought were good friends vanished, but people I hardly knew started packing up the house for me. They brought meals and offered to watch the children.

A church group from another part of town came over the day we had to move, rented the moving van, loaded it, drove it to our new place, unloaded it, and cleaned up the old house. Then they presented us with a "love offering" of enough money to help us get started in the new direction we felt God was leading us.

The challenges continued. Losing an eye meant losing depth perception and balance, so I had to re-learn how to do many, many things I had never before realized relied on hand-eye coordination, balance, and depth perception. This was a very long, fearful process, but I had to keep going because life didn't slow down just because I had been injured. Children needed caring for, a household needed managing, and a business needed me to write catalogs, speak at conventions, and exhibit at book fairs. There were times during those first years after the accident when I was hanging on emotionally and spiritually by the thinnest of threads.

But you know what? As trying as these times were, something "ground zero" about God was being formed in me. Francis Shaeffer always described our relationship with God "as a series of bows." Well, I had to bow to God's god-ness. This meant I had to acknowledge that He is God and I'm not. It's hard to explain, but I realized that God is God, so He's always right, no matter what happens and no matter what I might think about what He does. It may not make sense, but it was very freeing to know my life was out of my control and in the hands of a God "whose work is perfect and all His ways are just."

Several months after the surgery, I went for one of my monthly doctor's appointments and happened to sit in the waiting room next to a man who had also lost his eye. I asked him what had helped him get through it and he told me his story. He had been a telephone workman repairing the line when the pole he was attached to snapped at the base and fell over on him. The whole right side of his body had been crushed and he had undergone multiple surgeries to regain limited use of his limbs and to reconstruct his face. This is what he said, "For the first few months to a year, all you will be able to think about is what happened to you and how bad off you are. Then, after about a year, you'll only think about it a few times a day. After about another year, you'll only think about it a couple of times a week, then a couple of times a month, and then you'll get on with your life and hardly ever think about it anymore." After several years, I can say that the man was right.

There is one "final gift" I want to mention. One of my greatest private griefs in losing an eye was that I found I couldn't ride a horse anymore because I would get dizzy and lose my balance. I struggled with feeling like one of the things I loved to do most had been stripped from me. Then, in the fall of 1999 I went to a Cowboys for Christ service at the All-American Quarter Horse Congress. One of the men who spoke at the service (Steve Heckaman) had been a famous horse trainer who was involved in a horrendous traffic accident that crushed the right side of his body, killed his wife, and injured his young son. He had to undergo multiple surgeries and extensive rehabilitation. On that day in Cowboy Church he shared how the accident had totally transformed his life and brought him to Christ. He had learned to walk again, but one of his biggest challenges had been riding again because he had lost his right eye and no longer had the balance and depth perception he needed to stay in the saddle. With the help of friends, he learned to ride again and came back to the show ring and won at the largest Quarter Horse show in the world.

So guess what? I'm starting to ride again. I'm still scared, and it's still a struggle, but I'm going to do it. So what's the point of all this. Well, one point is that your "ground zero" experience may be the turning point in someone else's life. Another point is that "ground zero" experiences will eventually enter the "This too shall pass" phase and life will move on. The third point is that there will always be someone else whose "ground zero" experiences make yours look like a piece of cake. The fourth point is that, after a "ground zero" experience, life's everyday hassles don't seem so hard to bear. And the final point is that these experiences can be "gifts" in disguise, gifts that bring you face to face with Who God really is.

In Closing

I know this article is way too long, and I've turned it into a testimonial, but before closing I want to share a recent experience. My father died unexpectedly in November. Our grief was intense, but the funeral was a family celebration of his life and faith in God. Our son James sang one of Papa's favorite hymns, Chris and I both spoke and shared memories of his life, and his grand-daughter read a poem she had written.

During the preparations for my father's funeral, I began thinking about my grandmother, Caroline Blackshear Bridges. When she died nearly 25 years ago, I drove to Blakely, Georgia for her funeral. As I looked around me at her children, grandchildren, and great grand-children, as well as all the friends who had assembled in the Blakely First Baptist Church to pay their respects to the woman we had all called "Miss Carrie," I thought about Exodus 20: 5 that says "God visits the sins of the fathers upon the children to the third and fourth generation." I was suddenly struck with the reality that the reverse of that scripture is also true. God blesses the children of the righteous to the third and fourth generation. I knew that Miss Carrie had been a Christian. Her father died when she was a child, but her maternal grandfather was a Christian who said he received a call from God to become a missionary to the then wild and sparsely settled portions of backwoods Georgia. His name was James C. Bass, and he would travel to remote lumber camps and stand on a stump to preach the gospel to the rough lumberjacks. This grandfather had a powerful impact on Miss Carrie's life.

So there I was at my grandmother's funeral, over half a century after James C. Bass died, realizing that nearly every one of Miss Carrie's children, grandchildren, and great-grandchildren were Christians. As I sat through that funeral, I was overcome with gratitude for my godly heritage.

Then, this November I was at my father's funeral (Miss Carrie's son). I again saw children, grandchildren, and great-grandchildren: three generations who had all been affected by my father's belief in God. My father was not only a Christian, he was a Southern gentleman, who imparted a legacy of loyalty, integrity, principle, productivity, and confidence to his children, grandchildren, and great-grandchildren, as well as to all those around him. He gave us all a firm belief that each person's life could count for something. I spoke at my father's funeral, and what I shared was that God is faithful to bless righteousness. One righteous person can impact four generations, and those four generations can each impact four generations after them, so that the ongoing impact of righteousness can be never-ending as it passes down into the future. In fact, the Bible tells us God shows His mercy and steadfast love to a thousand generations of those who love Him and keep His commandments (Exodus 20:6).

How about that? We can bring mercy and steadfast love to a thousand generations simply by loving God and keeping His commandments.

So, I guess what I want to tell each of you who reads this article is: your life can affect forever. Maybe you don't have generations of godliness standing behind you, but you can start where you are and affect your children, grandchildren, and great-grandchildren at least three generations beyond you. And each of them can affect at least three generations beyond them. And who knows? If God were once willing to spare Sodom for only ten righteous men, maybe your presence in your own city has more of an impact than you could ever imagine.

Disclaimer I know this article tends to sound like I've got it all together. Nothing could be farther from the truth. It's only by God's grace that I am a fairly sane woman today, so I feel somewhat hypocritical in writing this article.

What makes me bold enough to write it is that I used to love listening to John Wimber, founder of the Vineyard Fellowships. Wimbers life impacted thousands, but every time he spoke he freely acknowledged there was nothing in him of any worth. He would often say, "I'm just a fat man trying to get to heaven." Well, I'm a lot like that. Theres nothing in me of any worth. Im just a frazzled, adventurous Mom trying to get to heaven.

Consider it a sheer gift, friends, when tests and challenges come at you from all sides. You know that under pressure your faith-life is forced into the open and shows its true colors. So don't try to get out of anything prematurely. Let it do its work so you become mature and well-developed, not deficient in any way.

> *"If you don't know what you're doing, pray to the Father. He loves to help. You'll get his help, and won't be condescended to when you ask for it. Ask boldly, believingly, without a second thought."*
>
> James 1: 1- 5, *The Message Bible*

19

MOM THE ROARING LION

"WHAT HAPPENED THAT I have become a drill sergeant in my own home?" "Why do I seem to be yelling at my kids all the time?" "Why do the children respond to their Dad but not to me?" Mothers ask me these questions virtually everywhere I speak. If you can say, "Yes, these are my questions, too," then the following may help you.

More often than not, Mom comes to homeschooling long before Dad. So, when Mom says to Dad, "Honey, I think we should home-school the children," Dad's response is often, "Sure, honey, go ahead." But, as long as having the children home is only Mom's idea, the out-working of this decision remains her responsibility until Dad comes around. Even then, Dad often does little more than support his wife.

PRINCIPLE 1 | GOD GIVES AUTHORITY TO DAD, NOT MOM
I cannot prove this with specific scriptures, but there are many evidences of this principle in a family setting. First, children normally respond to their fathers more readily than they do their mothers, and not just because Dad is physically more powerful. Children innately sense that Dad carries an authority that should be respected. Of course, this authority can be undermined either by Mom's attitude toward

Dad or by Dad's own behavior, especially illegitimate anger.

Second, Dad has the ability to "legitimize". By this I mean that children soon learn that some things are important to Dad while others are not. It's as if Dad has the power to give or withhold his "seal of approval". If he likes to watch Monday night football, the kids will likely grow up with this same interest. If Dad is not all that involved or seems disinterested in Mom's homeschooling efforts, the kids will grow up with an increasing tendency to give Mom a difficult time as she tries to teach them.

The quickest way to find out what's going on in a family is to ask Mom, "Do your children respond to you when you speak to them? Or, will they obey you only when your voice reaches a certain decibel level or because you have said the same thing a certain number of times?" The answer to these questions tells us whether or not Mom exercises ""false"" authority in her home.

PRINCIPLE 2 | WITHOUT AUTHORITY, MOM MUST CREATE A FALSE SENSE OF AUTHORITY

Mom must convince the children that they may be in danger if they don't do what she says. She does this by creating an atmosphere of fear.

We see this in Scripture. Satan has no authority. Jesus said, "All authority has been given to Me." That leaves no authority to Satan. Without authority, what can Satan do? He can go about like a roaring lion (2 Timothy 4:17). In other words, since he has no authority at all, he must try to scare us. And, whenever he succeeds in making us afraid, what he has actually done is make us submit to him in that area where we are fearful. Fear arises from the belief that God will not protect us or deliver us. Instead, we believe that Satan has authority in some area of our lives to do us harm. By becoming fearful, we submit to Satan's way to get out of our perceived trouble.

Jesus spent a lot of time talking about fear and giving many reasons why fear is inappropriate for anyone who knows the Lord. Human beings hate fear and will do just about anything to remove it from their lives. So Satan goes about, roaring like a lion, scaring us into thinking he can harm us, when he really has no authority to do us any harm at all.

DON'T SUPPORT YOUR WIFE'S HOMESCHOOLING EFFORTS. IF YOU DO, SHE WILL PROBABLY BURN OUT.

Take this principle into the home. When Mom has not been given the authority she needs to do her job, she must use whatever tactics work. She needs the children to obey so the day can move as smoothly as possible. But lacking the authority to make the kids obey, she must make them believe that she is able to do them some sort of harm (i.e. take away privileges, spank them, etc.). As long as the kids are afraid of her, she is obeyed. But eventually children grow up and begin to wonder why they should be afraid of someone who can only threaten and make noise. So, Mom yells louder. She makes stronger threats.

This is not real authority. And, when the kids realize Mom can't really harm them, they begin to ignore or develop a hatred toward, their own mother.

PRINCIPLE 3 | DAD MUST GIVE HIS AUTHORITY TO MOM
Obviously, parents have a Scriptural mandate to discipline their children. When the children are very young, discipline should take place quickly before the child forgets what he did that required the discipline. However, as children grow older, discipline can wait for an

appropriate time and can be given by the appropriate parent. In my opinion, the appropriate parent should be Dad and not Mom, especially in the case of boys. There comes a time when Mom should let go of disciplining the children, particularly boys. Boys should not grow up having to be overpowered by a woman (yelled at and threatened), especially by the one woman in their young lives whose words they should respect.

Dads have the capacity to set an atmosphere in the home where his presence is felt even though he is not present. He can do this by giving his authority to his wife. Mom should never have to raise her voice or resort to saying something several times or to manipulation before her children respond to her. The very fact that she has spoken to them should be enough for them to respond. Of course, they could always respectfully ask, "May I do such and such first?" Or, "Would it be all right if I did what you are asking later or in a different way?" If done without manipulation, this is acceptable. The point is, Mom should never have to become a "roaring lion". There is only one person who does this. It is the person who has no authority.

So, what's Dad to do? First, realize that you carry an authority in the home that God has given you. It will not be given to anyone else. Second, understand that God is not going to one day visit your wife and give her a final exam as to how the children have turned out. If He is going to visit anyone, it is going to be you. So, don't support your wife's homeschooling efforts. If you do, she will probably burn out. It is not biblical for you to support your wife's homeschooling. Rather, it is biblical for her to support your homeschooling.

Does this mean you begin doing the work she has been doing? No. I'm not talking about work. I'm talking about responsibility. You are the one responsible in God's eyes; so be responsible. Wives burn out, not because of the work they do, but because of the responsibility they carry. If your wife is feeling responsible for how her homeschooling efforts turn out, this is not appropriate. You, Dad, have probably made her feel as if she is on probation. Take that feeling off her shoulders. You are in charge whether you like it or not. Say to her, "Ultimately, I am the one responsible for how our children turn out. I must be involved in every aspect of the upbringing of our children, especially their homeschooling. Now, let's see how you can best help me do that."

Finally, Dads, do what it takes for you and your wife to get on the same page about how you intend to raise the children. Then, sit everyone down and explain what a typical day is going to look like. You are legitimizing your wife's workday. You are authorizing your wife's activities. You are giving her your authority to act on your behalf. Make it clear that she is helping you do what both of you have decided to do. This is the critical point. Also make it clear that when Mom speaks, the children should respond. And, if they don't, Mom is not responsible for making them obey. She is only responsible for telling them what Dad and she have agreed upon.

What do I mean by the words, "Mom is not responsible for making them obey?" In our home, if the children won't respond to their mother, then Mom is free to take a nap, read a book, take a walk, or whatever else she wants to do. It's up to Dad (me) to make sure the kids respond to Mom. Many Dad's don't want to come home from a hard day's work and deal with relational issues in their home. I would like to say, "That's understandable. You are tired and deserve some peace and quiet when you come home from 'slaying dragons' all day." But, the truth is, this is your responsibility; your "high calling" so to speak. It is what you get to do.

Whenever I share this material in one of my seminars, someone asks, "What if my husband isn't interested in helping me in the ways you have suggested?" If your husband will read an article, I suggest you ask him to read this one. The only other thing I can say is that God has promised to send the "spirit of Elijah" to turn the hearts of the fathers to their children and the hearts of the children to their fathers. It was this very scripture that caused us to name our business "The Elijah Company". Pray for this spirit to fall on your husband. It is God's desire more than it is yours.

DAD HAS THE ABILITY TO "LEGITIMIZE".

The other question I am usually asked is, "I am a single Mom. What do I do about authority?" This is an even more complex problem because I firmly believe that the Church has overlooked its mandated responsibility to act as an extended family for one another, especially for the children. We are all to be brothers and sisters to one another as well as surrogate "parents" (moms and dads, uncles & aunts) to all the children. I pray that the Body of Christ will begin to turn to the many unfathered children and give some level of fatherhood to them. When a child believes that a man cares for him or her, that man has earned the right to say, "Now, son, the way you are treating your mother is not acceptable..." May we begin to turn our attention to helping these single Moms who need our input into the lives of their children.

My Dad died when I was two years old. I know what it is like to be a boy with no father in his life. My uncles and aunts all had young families and were busy. Although that was decades ago I can remember virtually every time a family invited me to join them on an outing or vacation. I needed this desperately. There are a lot of fatherless children out there who need surrogate dads and uncles. If the Church won't help here, who will?

Remember, however, there is always a father figure in a child's life, whether that child is you, or your own child. Recently a single mom told me, "I know that, for my children, if the Dad steps back, my children will default to their 'higher' father figure: their Heavenly Father who has promised to be a father to the fatherless."

Principle 4 | Dad, the Roaring Lion

I have seen dads lead their families with anger. I have one thing to say about this: A father's anger is so damaging, there is seldom a time when it could be considered legitimate. Of course we all know that scripture tells us to be angry, but not to sin. However, leading your family with anger is one sure way to lose all the authority God has given you as a man.

Principle 5 | Giving Mom Authority May Not Solve the Problem

I cannot end this article without saying that if tension exists between the kids and Mom, giving Mom the authority she needs will not relieve this tension until you both understand why God is bringing children home. In many of our other articles as well as the seminars we give, my wife and I have tried to explain some of the reasons why having our children home during the day is sometimes not as positive an experience as parents had hoped. If this is your situation, you may obtain our seminar materials and listen to them.

Until the time when Dad can be home during most of the waking hours of his children, the family must find ways to make sure his presence is felt, though he is absent in body.

20

IN MAY, 2002, OUR 17-YEAR-OLD son graduated from high school. This was the fourth of our five children to graduate from home school. It was hard for us to believe that we had been on this journey for over 20 years! While there have been some bumps in the road, for the most part we have thoroughly enjoyed the ride.

As parents, we've been "in school" for all these years, too. I can honestly say we've learned as much or more than our children! We've found some of the "lessons" to be rather challenging, and some of the "courses" we found ourselves enrolled in were much more rigorous than we had anticipated! But my husband and I agree that we wouldn't trade the opportunity we've had to be with our children during these years for anything in the world. Watching them grow in knowledge and experience and in love for God and one another has brought us a satisfaction and joy that's hard to describe. We've made many mistakes-but we learned early on that mistakes are often our best learning opportunities in disguise!

So, how do you "do" high school at home? I wish I could answer this question. I had to figure out with each of our children what their individual high school experiences should look like. Our son, Peter followed a fairly typical college-prep curriculum. Liz had some severe health issues that had to be taken into consideration. Kimberly needed a totally kinesthetic learning environment to succeed. Andrew was extremely "left-brained" and therefore totally comfortable with textbooks, but needed a lot of nurturing to develop his creative skills. Joel is musically talented and academically "gifted." We are in the process of figuring out what his high school years might look like. The biggest lesson we've learned along the way is that our Heavenly Father has a vested interest in our children's education. When we don't know what to do or which direction to head in, He graciously opens the right doors at the right time. We've learned to be totally dependent upon Him, and we look to Him as our "home schooling expert" in residence. These are just a few of the principles He has taught us:

Principle 1 | It's Not About Curriculum!

If we've learned anything in our many years of home schooling, it is this: academics are the least important element in a successful home school. OK, I know this is shocking and perhaps even heretical, but we have found it to be true. We have learned that home schooling is all about relationships! If the relationship between parent and child/child and sibling(s) is strained, home schooling is not an enjoyable pursuit! This is especially true during the high school years!

We have come to recognize that puberty is God's gift to us as parents. It is yet another opportunity to forge the relational bonds between our children and us, and preparing them to be valuable members of our families, churches and communities. I firmly believe that during puberty we get the first strong glimpses of who God has created each child to be in His Kingdom. Sometimes, that looks very different from the person we thought this person was supposed to be. Most of the tensions that erupt during adolescence are due, I think, to us trying to fit our children into a mold that is not meant for them.

I learned this the hard way. Because I had successfully prepared Peter, our oldest son (who possessed a temperament and interests that were very like my own) for college, I thought I could just reproduce the same course of study for each of our children. I quickly learned that what worked for our visual, fine-arts-loving, history-devouring, can't- read-enough-books-fast-enough, oldest child would not work for his siblings. Due to space limitations in this article, may I just say, this was a painful revelation for me? I realized that most of the problem I was running into with our teen-aged children was due to my lack of recognition of who they were! I needed to change my goals and programs to fit their needs.

LEARN TO LISTEN WITHOUT CONDEMNING, AND LEARN TO RESPOND TO THEIR THOUGHTS WITHOUT FEELING LIKE YOU HAVE TO WIN THE DEBATE.

This requires a lot of talking. Well, to be honest, this requires a lot of listening on our part. I find that as I make room for my children to express their opinions and thoughts and feelings, that we generally end up on friendly turf, even if we don't totally agree with one another. Our children also know that they can talk with us about anything, and that they can say anything to us as long as they speak respectfully.

Adolescents need room to try out new ideas and thoughts. It is their way of coming to an understanding of who they really are and what they really believe. We had to learn to calmly listen to them as they sometimes said things that we totally disagreed with. Sometimes as parents, we fail to give our children the room to go through this process. We immediately chide them for foolishness, or we are quick to condemn them for their lack of biblical thinking. This is a sure way to keep your children from sharing their thoughts and ideas with you in the future. Learn to listen without condemning, and learn to respond to their thoughts without feeling like you have to win the debate. This brings us to the second principle for successfully home schooling the older child:

PRINCIPLE 2 | DON'T WIN THE BATTLE; WIN THE WAR

It is an absolute mystery to me how my progeny could be so completely different from either my spouse or myself. For instance, I like to study in absolute silence. I also like to have everything around me neat and organized. This is my best mode for learning and for living. How can it be, then, that out of our 5 children, not a single one enjoys this type of study/living environment? For years, I battled with my children over messy rooms, studying while sprawled out on the bed, eating while studying, listening to music while studying, etc. We had some rather heated encounters over these issues. Then, one day, it was as though a light came on: my children were different from me. And, I needed to give them the freedom to be who they were. After all, it wasn't exactly a moral issue that they liked to listen to music while they studied! And, if they were happy in a room that seemed to be messy to me, why should it bother me? The whole rest of the house was my domain! Couldn't I just close the door and leave it at that? I had to learn how to negotiate with my children. We didn't give up our parental authority and adopt a "peace at any price" lifestyle, but we did find that when we said, "yes" to as much as we possibly could, our "nos" carried a lot more weight and met a lot less resistance. We did not compromise on moral issues, but we did have to realize that not everything was a moral issue.

PRINCIPLE 3 | GIVE THEM ROOTS; BUT GIVE THEM WINGS, TOO

I think the hardest part of parenting older children is the pain of letting go of control over every aspect of their lives. We've worked so hard to instill our values and morals in our children that we cringe at the thought of letting them fail or make mistakes. We are so highly invested in their lives and their education that when they succeed, we feel successful. Conversely, when they fail, we feel like failures. When our kids are little, they try to do everything to please us. When they begin to come into adulthood, the person they were created to be comes into focus. Sometimes, we have a hard time giving our children the freedom to be that person.

I learned this lesson when Kimberly entered adolescence. She was a highly kinesthetic learner and a strong-willed individual. Everything about us seemed to clash. We went through months of tears and harsh words and outright anger with one another. I was certain that her life was going to shipwreck, and I had no clue how to stop it from happening. One day, as I was praying yet another prayer for her to change, I felt the Lord speak to me in my heart. What He impressed upon me rocked my world. "She's fine," He said. "She's exactly who I created her to be. You are the one who needs to change." I didn't like it one bit, but this revelation was forcing me to recognize that I was trying to make my daughter be who I thought she should be, and I was totally missing the wonderful person God had made her to be. I repented. Not just to the Lord, but to my daughter. I had to learn to appreciate her for who she was. She didn't like books. She didn't like academics. She didn't share my taste in clothing. She didn't like classical music. Somewhere during adolescence, I had begun to interpret these differences in our personalities as negatives. But God was shining a whole new light on who Kimberly was, and I had to learn to see her the way He did. Part of my "homework" during this time was to find 3 things every day (and they had to be different each time) that I liked about my daughter. This may sound silly, but it was not easy for me to do. I had become so accustomed to being disappointed with Kimberly that I was dangerously unaware of the many charming aspects of her unique and vibrant personality. I had to learn how to be Kimberly's advocate instead of her adversary.

One of the ways we went about doing this was to give Kimberly more control in the area of her education. This seemed like a huge risk to us. What if the experiment failed and she left high school both unemployed and unprepared for college? My husband and I decided that we needed to trust Kimberly and give her the opportunity to pursue her passions. Not fond of academics, my daughter needed a lot of "real life" opportunities to learn from. Her high school years contained an absolute minimum of formal curriculum. Instead, they were filled with volunteer positions, part-time jobs, keeping the family garden, cooking, mission trips, homegrown businesses, leadership in her youth group and home school support group, working with children, and anything that had to do with drama and music. During her senior year, she was offered a part-time job in a local medical practice. In this position, she learned bookkeeping, filing, billing and how to run the front desk. When she mastered something on the job, she asked to be taught something new, and finally, at the tender age of 17 she became responsible for every aspect of the insurance end of the practice. This soon became a full-time position.

She learned more from this job than from any academic course I could have planned for her. She now works for a private insurance/investment firm in our area. She has enormous responsibilities, and her boss is absolutely thrilled with her! The part of her temperament that nearly drove me crazy during her teen years is the very quality that makes her so successful in her work: she won't take "no" for an answer. Because of her tenacity, she ensures that clients receive all the benefits they are due from their insurance companies. She is also gifted at closing a deal, and problem solving. I can also see how these character traits will serve her well in her missionary calling in the Kingdom of God! How thankful I am that I changed before our relationship was destroyed! She is one of my favorite people in the whole world, and we enjoy a warm and loving friendship based on trust and mutual respect.

PRINCIPLE 4 | WHAT WORKS AT HOME WORKS IN THE "REAL" WORLD, TOO
I know I sound like a broken record, but I have to say it again. Academics are the smallest element in high school success. We have seen that the values and training received in the home transfer seamlessly into college or work. The hours spent training a child to mow the lawn or clean the kitchen or care for younger siblings are the very lessons that prepare them for work and for school. Home schoolers often tend to give greater weight and concern to books and tests and curriculum, but we have seen first hand that it is the character training, skill development, and real life experience found in the home that makes our children truly successful in life!

Our children have excelled in both college and work. But it is not because we enrolled them in the most rigorous academic programs available. We decided to place a heavier emphasis on equipping our children with tools for living than on merely filling their heads with academic content and information. It seems radical, but we have seen that training our children to express themselves well in spoken and written word, giving them plenty of practice at researching and finding answers for themselves, instilling in them the importance of treating all people with dignity and respect, and giving them plenty of opportunity to learn to carry out a task with excellence from beginning to completion is the very best high school curriculum available, regardless of career choice! Our children left our home confident in their ability to tackle just about any situation. If they didn't know how to do something, they knew how to ask the right questions and where to find the right information. They had learned how to handle conflict and difficult personalities, how to relate well to people older than themselves and to people younger than themselves. They understood the importance of doing a job to the best of their abilities.

Through experience, they also learned how to properly manage their finances. In their early years, we opted to sometimes let our children make a poor financial decision. We wanted them to learn that money is easily spent but difficult to retrieve. We also wanted them to discover that today's "treasure" is tomorrow's trash. Each of our children has worked part-time during high school. We made sure they understood how to set up and maintain a budget and balance a checking account. We also demonstrated and let them experience the joy of giving.

It is amazing to see how hard credit card companies work in order to lure a young adult into mountains of credit-induced debt! This is perhaps one of the areas of education most neglected by even the best of public and private schools. Make sure your young adults know how to avoid this snare, and you will be doing them the biggest favor of their lives!

Amazing doors of opportunity have opened for our children. I think this is mostly due to the character training and practical experience they received in our home, our community and our church. They have been placed in positions of responsibility and authority that are unusual for people their age. It was not curriculum or academics that prepared them to meet these challenges; it was the stuff of real living that made them ready for adulthood. How do I handle extended illness during high school?

Our oldest daughter, Liz, became severely ill during tenth grade. We had dutifully charted out a college prep course for her, but it soon became apparent that her illness left her with little energy to pursue such a rigorous course. Once again, we had to listen to her and adjust our plans to fit her energy level and her circumstances.

The biggest challenge during this time was not keeping her well physically; it was the battle against depression that was the hardest to win. We had to constantly encourage her in the Lord. My husband and I and her siblings spent countless hours playing, talking to and loving her. We had to help her see that her illness did not define who she was as a person. We helped her to do this by releasing her to pursue her interests.

She was fascinated with World War II and read anything she could get her hands on that dealt with this subject. Since she showed a natural talent for art, we enlisted a friend who was gifted in the arts to give her watercolor lessons. She also enjoyed sewing when her energy levels were good, so we hired a friend to come to our house and teach her to sew. She made many beautiful gifts for friends and family using this ability. The piano was a source of satisfaction for her, but her illness often prevented her from taking regular lessons. There were days and sometimes even weeks when just living used up most of her energy. During these times, she read and listened to many books on tape. We rented historical videos for her to watch. By the end of her junior year, her health was improved, but we had not accomplished a lot in the area of academics! I was very worried about these "lost" years in her education, but was pleasantly surprised when her end of the year tests, which were required by our state, came back looking really good! Evidently, she had learned more than we realized during this very difficult time.

About halfway through 11th grade, Liz told us that she had no desire to go to college. Since Peter had gone to a private university on a handsome scholarship, this was hard for me to handle. You look successful as a home school parent when you can tell your friends and family that your child has won a college scholarship. You look less successful when your daughter winds up working at a grocery store as a cashier! What is fine as a part-time job during high school is less than stellar as a career choice! It was a real test of our trust in our daughter and in the Lord to let Liz choose to keep her job at the grocery store even after she graduated from high school.

Liz worked in grocery stores for over a year, filling different positions. She seemed to enjoy the contact with people, and she loved the fact that she was able to buy her first car (used) with her earnings. One day while I was taking care of some banking for our family business, I noticed that the branch was short-handed. When I found that they were hiring, I encouraged our daughter to ask for an interview. She had great people skills, and her experience handling cash at the grocery store and her natural attention to detail would make her an excellent teller, I thought. So did the bank! They hired her immediately! She worked first as a teller, and then the bank paid her to take some classes and promoted her to a supervisory position. This was on the job training, and Liz thrived on it. After a year in this position, she decided she wanted to take a leave of absence, receive some further spiritual training and go on a mission trip. The bank held her position open for her so she was able to pursue this dream.

Upon her return from this adventure, Liz was promoted to a position in the corporate office of this bank. This is a position that generally requires a degree, but because she had proven herself in her previous post, they gave her the job anyway. She spends much of her spare time volunteering in various ministries in our local church. Once again, we are amazed at the doors the Lord has opened for Liz in spite of her years of illness and without a college degree! We know that much of the maturity, sensitivity and character she possesses were forged during the physical struggles she endured during her high school years.

What it's really all about? As you can see from our story, there's no one "right" way to complete a high school education at home. The way I see it, our primary job as home educators is to take the time to identify the gifts and callings in each of our children's lives. Then, we can research and educate ourselves to be the best possible facilitator for our child's education. We can line up activities, job opportunities, life experiences, and educational resources that will help each child discover their personal passion and achieve their highest personal potential.

We have found the high school years to be a wonderful time to cement values, build relationships and reap the harvest from the seeds we diligently sowed during our children's early years. My only complaint about educating my children through high school is that the time passed too quickly! My husband and I are thankful every day that we did not squander these few precious years on unnecessary conflict and endless academics. It's not that we feel that we did everything just right, but we do feel that we focused on the things that really mattered in the light of eternity.

Our children are becoming adults in their own right. They are joyfully serving God, skillfully serving His creation, and continuing their education in their own individual ways. Our lives are richer because of the love we share with them, and the many things they have taught us. We can hardly wait for the unveiling of the next adventure the Father has planned for each one of them!

About the author of "Educating the Older Child" | *Dale and Kathy Clement live in North Carolina with their 5 children, ages-26. They embraced the homeschool lifestyle more than 20 years ago. Dale and his two oldest sons are partners in the family-owned small business. Kathy is co-moderator of the Elijah Company's discussion board, Elijah Counsel at www.elijahcompany.com. They also host a home-based church. Along with homeschooling their 13 year old son, Kathy enjoys encouraging other homeschool moms, writing, public speaking, reading, working in the kitchen, traveling, and spending time with her family.*

ABOUT THE BOOKS WE SELL.... We don't carry everything available for home schoolers. We've limited our selections to materials we have used with our own children or to items friends we trust rave about that are educationally sound. This way we can stand behind each product and say, "It works!" We're aware of a lot of educational junk food out there that does nothing to nourish young minds and hearts. We are also aware that home schooling has become an industry and many people with no interest in home schoolers are beginning to cash in on this market. We believe home schooling is part of a move of God to restore the family, and we don't want to merchandise what God is doing, we want to service it.

ELIJAHCOMPANY.COM WEBSITE

Why visit us online? There are over 2000 good reasons—our website features our entire product line with pictures and current inventory status. Plus, you can order any time, find out about special promotions, read in-depth homeschooling articles, discuss topics with other home schooling parents, sign up for future catalogs and more.

EJOURNAL

Why not join us? The 20,000 home educators who receive our EJournal newsletter get timely, new articles, promotional specials, company news and more delivered right to their email inbox. We offer many articles and thought-provoking essays through the EJournal that we just can't fit into the catalog. Best of all, it's free. Sign up for it at ElijahCompany.com. And, rest assured we never sell, rent or share our customer email or mailing list with anyone for any reason.

ELIJAH COUNSEL

What do the numbers 2000 and 20 have in common? That's the number of members and discussion forums that have clicked with Elijah Counsel and are swapping ideas, asking questions and encouraging each other in their homeschooling journey. Our moderators are Christian homeschooling mothers with a wealth of experience and a big heart to help you as you raise your children at home. Membership is free and all you have to do is go to ElijahCompany.com and click on Counsel to start using this great resource.

ELIJAH CONFERENCES AND SEMINARS

What could we possibly speak about at a conference that isn't already being offered? Our passion is to help families raise their children in their homes. Catalogs, websites, travel and discussion boards are just some of the ways we serve you. But there's nothing like talking with you face to face. And we like to do more than just talk about topics and issues relevant to your homeschooling experience, we actually offer on-site prayer at conferences as long as the schedule permits.

Typically, we will speak on topics God is placing on our heart as we see Him moving within the homeschooling movement. You can read more about each particular seminar on our website. We also have past seminars on Science, History, Learning Styles and more available on CD through our online store. If you are interested in helping us put on a conference in your area, please email us at chris@elijahco.com or give us a call. We also welcome international speaking engagements.

ELIJAH TRAVEL

We have been working with several worldwide travel agencies to offer home schoolers the opportunity to explore history through travel by studying about the Old and New Testaments, Ancient Egypt, Ancient Greece, Rome, the Middle Ages, the Renaissance and Reformation, and Modern European History by actually visiting the places where history happened. We will make the trips fun and educational.

We offer packages of study materials for a historical period and then take home schoolers and their parents on an in-depth, on-site tour with an expert in that historical period. We also hope to be able to have a university grant college credit for high schoolers who work through the study materials and take the trip.

For our Intimate Israel Tour, Elijah Company, in association with Heartland Tours of Israel, has created a unique chronological journey that, as much as possible, follows the Bible in chronological order from Abraham's first encounter with God to modern day Israel. We spend a day with the homeschoolers of Israel, and residents of settlements and Kibbutzim. We place biblical and current events in their historical and geographic context as we visit Israel's Holocaust Museum, raft the Jordan River and enjoy authentic Israeli meals.

If you think you may be interested in these opportunities check out ElijahCompany.com and click on Travel for the latest information on the Intimate Israel Tour and future destinations.

MANY OF YOU HAVE asked about us—who we are; what we are like; what we believe; why we carry the products we do (and don't carry others). We hope this biographical sketch will answer your questions.

The Elijah Company began as the Davis family. Chris (Dad) grew up in Los Angeles and came to the Southeast at 15 when his mother died. (His father had died when Chris was two.) Chris attended the University of Georgia and received a B.A. in Business Administration and for years owned a construction equipment rental business. Ellyn (Mom) grew up in Atlanta, attended Georgia State and Emory Universities, earned a B.S. and M.S. and completed all but the dissertation for her Ph.D. in Microbiology/Biochemistry. After Chris and Ellyn married, they both became committed Christians. God eventually led Chris to sell his business, earn a Master's degree in counseling, and become a pastor.

We had hoped to have many children, and left the family planning to the Lord, but His timing has been different than ours and we now have four on earth and two in heaven. Catrina, our eldest, is a Social Worker in Atlanta where she lives with her husband, John, and two boys, Josh and Jake. We became interested in keeping our kids at home (instead of sending them to school) as we cried out to the Lord over problems we saw Catrina have in school. In 1981 a friend gave us Raymond Moore's book, *Home Grown Kids*, and a conviction was deeply planted in us that has never wavered.

Our three boys have never known an institutionalized school setting. From the beginning we understood that boys needed to spend a lot of time outdoors, exploring, collective, observing, building, working with animals and giving as much expression to their personal interests as possible.

Seth, our oldest, left home in 2001 to attend the Bethel School of Ministry in Redding, California. As of this writing he is full-time on the church's staff. As Seth grew up he spent lots of time outdoors and soaked up anything having to do with nature. At 13 he was building and designing model rockets. At 14 he had developed a program for the Internet which was used all over the world. At 15 he was hired to assist the professor in teaching a computer science class at the local junior college. By the time Seth had left home he had performed in numerous musical theater productions, was a decent pianist, a good basketball player, had taught himself several computer languages, was considered to be one of the premier young male tap dancers in the country, and had been offered a scholarship at a top university. Today, when he is not working or at church, you will find him snow boarding with his friends.

James left home in 2001 to attend the Bethel School of Ministry with his brother. He currently divides his time between Kansas City and his hometown and is establishing his own entrepreneurial base. James began acting at age 10, and has worked professionally for several years. His great love is dance. James was also a champion horseback rider, winning both the State 4-H and Tennessee Quarter Horse Championships.

Blake opened in his first musical theater presentation at age 8. By 15 he was a professional actor. For years his passion has been the Middle Ages which he studies whenever he has a spare moment, which is not often. When Blake discovered a fear of heights, he became an ardent rock climber which he has integrated into his Venture Crew

Scouting experience. Blake began his own business at age 17.

We started the Elijah Company about 15 years ago when we found it impossible to get good teaching materials. Believe it or not, there was once a day when nobody would sell to home schoolers. Whenever we found something we really liked we would buy a few copies for our friends. Our intention was to use the business as a means of traveling and working together as a family; never expecting it to provide enough income to live on! But sales increased steadily.

When Chris had been pastoring for many years (and seeing very little of his family), God began strongly impressing him with the importance of the family, and particularly the importance of fatherhood. Chris struggled with his decision for over a year, and finally resigned from the pastorate because he felt God sending him home to raise his sons. This meant we had no source of income but our little business. We had named it "The Elijah Company" because we wanted the business to have the spirit of Elijah that prepares for the coming of the Lord by turning the hearts of the fathers to the children and the hearts of the children to their fathers (Malachi 4:5-6). Neither of us had any experience with the book business, and we've learned the hard way—by making mistakes. But God has been gracious. Although there have been tense times, our little business has grown and supported us all these years.